*By the hand of genius we are carried
to the most distant eras; we are not
dragged out from our brief lifespan.
Everyone gladly joins in conversation
of every age, from every age,
hand in hand with those from every age.
Let us turn from this brief and transient time
and offer our minds and hearts to the past,
which is long and eternal.*
  —Seneca, *On the Shortness of Life*

The Classics Cave
Sugar Land

The Classics Cave
the earliest light for a brighter life
www.theclassicscave.com

Are you looking for the best books ever? Or new ways to read and benefit from them? Let The Classics Cave be your guide!

The Classics Cave is an educational organization centered on the classics of antiquity, with an emphasis on Greece and Rome.

Our mission is to shine the light of the past into the present for a brighter life today.

Our goal is practice—the application of ancient wisdom and ways to our contemporary lives.

We publish books, develop and provide online materials, organize and do outreach, and produce and distribute a variety of print and other media intended to entertain and educate, cultivate and motivate.

Visit The Classics Cave online (www.theclassicscave.com) to support our mission and to access a growing catalog of engaging books, useful gear, and other helpful materials for individuals, educators, and all others interested in benefiting from ancient literature.

The Wisdom & Way
of The Cynics

Pocket Edition
The Wisdom & Way
of the Cynics

selected, introduced, and edited by
Tim J. Young

Cave Wisdom & Way Series
wisdom and ways for today

The Classics Cave
Sugar Land

The Wisdom & Way of the Cynics: Pocket Edition

Copyright © 2022 by Tim J. Young

All rights reserved. Accept for those "fair uses" provided for in U.S. copyright law, no part of this book may be reproduced or transmitted in any form or by any means, electronic or mechanical, including photocopying, recording, or by any information storage and retrieval system, without permission in writing from the copyright owner.

ISBN 978-1-943915-06-4

Published in the United States by
The Classics Cave
P.O. Box 19038
Sugar Land, TX 77496
contact@theclassicscave.com
www.theclassicscave.com

The Classics Cave is an educational organization centered on the classics of antiquity, with an emphasis on Greece and Rome. Our mission is to shine the light of the past into the present for a brighter life today. Our goal is practice—the application of ancient wisdom and ways to our contemporary lives. We publish books, develop and provide online materials, organize and do outreach, and produce and distribute a variety of print and other media intended to entertain and educate, cultivate and motivate.

Visit The Classics Cave online (www.theclassicscave.com) to support our mission and to access a growing catalog of engaging books, useful gear, and other helpful materials for individuals, educators, and all others who are interested in benefiting from ancient literature.

CONTENTS

Cave Wisdom & Way Series Introduction   11

INTRODUCTION   13

Sources & Abbreviations   17
for the Wisdom & Way of the Cynics

TOPICS WITH SELECTIONS

PART 1
The Cynic Way of Life

1. Doing Philosophy   23
2. The Cynic Way of Life   27
3. The Cynic Outfit   32

PART 2
Cynic Goals

4. The Goal of Life   41
5. Happiness   43
6. Virtue & Vice   47
7. Following Nature   52
8. Freedom   55

9. Reputation & Opinion ... 59
10. Actuality versus Appearance ... 63
11. Real Human Beings ... 66
12. Heroic Examples ... 68
13. The Wise & Good Man ... 72

Part 3
Cynic Training & Practice

14. Training & Practice ... 75
15. Soul-Care & Self-Reflection ... 82
16. Endurance ... 85
17. Hard Work ... 87
18. Suffering & Hardship ... 89
19. Desire & Desire Reduction ... 93
20. Self-Control ... 99
21. Sex & Sexual Desire ... 101
22. Pleasure ... 103
23. Self-Sufficiency & Contentment ... 107
24. Circumstances ... 111
25. Fortune, Chance, Luck (*Tychē*) ... 115
26. Wealth ... 117
27. Poverty ... 122
28. Things Indifferent ... 128
29. Simplicity, Frugality & Living Simply ... 129
30. Shamelessness & Rejection ... 137
31. Reinterpretation ... 141

32. Playing Your Role Well	143
33. Reason	144
34. Superstition	147
35. Death	149

PART 4

The Cynic Mission

36. Mission—Admonishing & Helping Others	155
37. Citizenship & Political Involvement	159
38. Frankness & Freedom of Speech	160
39. Delusion, Vanity, Emptiness	161
40. Altering the Currency	164
41. Friendship	165
Miscellaneous Sayings & Anecdotes	168

WAYS OF PRACTICE

—A Plan of Life Following the Cynics	175
—Ways of Practice Following the Cynics	179
—The Cynics Cave Sparks (Conversation Starters Sparked by the Cynics)	183
Will you help the Cave?	185
Looking for the best books ever?	186

Cave Wisdom & Way
Series Introduction

Those who make it their business to collect whatever is beneficial from every writing are like rivers that grow larger by taking in the flow of streams from every side. The poet Hesiod's saying about "adding little to little" is true not only for the accumulation of money but also for gathering together every kind of knowledge. —Basil the Great

If you were to gather together all of Greek and Latin literature, you would have hundreds of volumes filled with a variety of poetry and prose—works exploring every kind of knowledge and wisdom and proposing a whole range of ways to go in life.

Wisdom? Yes. Surveying these many volumes of epic and lyric poems, tragedies and comedies, histories, orations, philosophies, and more, you would soon notice the emphasis the ancients put on wisdom in the form of stories, observations, sayings, and anecdotes.

Why all the knowledge and wisdom? Certainly it wasn't for the sake of trivia. Rather, as the Athenian Niceratus put it relative to the wisdom of Homer, the point was to "develop into a good man." In other words, the *wisdom* was a *way*—a way of life, of practice. It was the path to achieve excellence, virtue, and every good and valuable thing tied to these.

Such a survey, though doubtlessly worthwhile, would take years to complete. It is the Cave's goal, therefore, to help you out. We've gathered what's best of the wisdom on offer and the many proposed ways of life. We've collected the stories, observations, sayings, and anecdotes, and have noted the most helpful practices. We've done this so that, as the philosopher Epicurus said, "We may keep in mind the principle teachings" and "practice those things that produce happiness."

The goal of the Wisdom & Way Series is to inspire beneficial ways of feeling, thinking, and acting. Though we wish to "hold fast to the ancients," as the philosopher Crates of Thebes advised, we have no desire to remain with the dead, as it were. Rather, the aim is to use their insights and practices to live a better life *right now*, while wisely and courageously moving toward the future.

As for the work you have in hand, we hope you will benefit from every bit of wisdom and trust you will use it to walk along a more excellent way.

How to read? Take your time. Ponder. Skip around. Commit what you like to memory. But most of all, practice.* For as the philosopher Diogenes of Sinope declared, "Practice has the power to conquer anything."

With these points in mind, welcome to the **Cave Wisdom & Way Series**.

---

*For guided practice, you may wish to use a book from the Cave Workbook & Journal Series.

Introduction*

THE CYNICS AND their way of life influenced the Greek and Roman worlds for centuries, from the rise and development of Cynicism around the end of the fifth and beginning of the fourth centuries BC to its demise sometime toward the fall of the western half of the Roman Empire in the late fifth century AD.

The philosopher Plato judged Diogenes of Sinope, the principal founder of ancient Cynicism, a "Socrates gone mad"—the Greek is *mainomenos*, a word related to the English words "mania" and "maniac."

His quip was not intended as a compliment. Rather, it was meant to undercut what Diogenes was doing. The man's crazy! insane! unhealthy! For Plato, Diogenes—and thus, Cynicism—was an extreme version of the far healthier, moderate, and *sane* Socrates.

If Diogenes was a Socrates *mainomenos*, then what was it that he and his wisdom and way of life took too far? Asked another way, What was Cynicism all about?

The Cynics practiced the Socratic art of endurance—Socrates' self-control and indifference to suffering. They also emphasized Socrates' frank and open search for the meaning of reality and human life, and his free questioning of conventional terms used to describe the same. Then there was their habitual inattention to their own appearance, and their emphasis on frugality and living a simple life. All of these, and more, Diogenes of Sinope and the other Cynics took to a *mainomenos* extreme in imitation of Socrates.

The ancient Stoics, who were the offspring of the Cynics, explained that "the Cynic philosophy and way of life is a shortcut to virtue." As such, it was a shortcut to happiness. The Stoic description is one that the tenth century AD Byzantine *Suda*—a historical dictionary and encyclopedia covering the ancient Greek, Roman, and Byzantine worlds—picked up on, one that will serve us well for our own brief "definition" of Cynicism:

> Cynicism: a school of philosophy. It's definition is "a short path to virtue." The goal of Cynicism is to live according to virtue, in the manner of Diogenes . . . The Cynics held that one should live frugally, eating sufficient food to support oneself and looking down on wealth and reputation and nobility of birth. Some of them were vegetarians, using plants for food, and they drank cold water and utilized whatever shelter they happened to find, even large wine-jars. They used to say that it was a unique characteristic of a god neither to need nor want anything—and those who need and want few things are like a god. They also hold that virtue is teachable, and that it cannot be lost.

The name itself—Cynic (*kunikos*) or Cynicism (*kunismos*)—comes from the Greek for dog (*kuōn* or *kyōn*).

Some of the most significant Cynics were Antisthenes of Athens, Diogenes of Sinope, and Crates of Thebes, as well as Crates' wife, Hipparchia of Maroneia, her brother Metrocles, Teles of Megara, Demetrius, Dio Chrysostom, and Demonax. They were known for their droll wit, their wry manner of speaking, and, well, their radical way of life. That said, they were quite earnest in helping others in their own approach to happiness and excellence or virtue.

More than a theoretical philosophy, Cynicism was a way of life. Cynic practice consisted of two major aspects. One aspect was concerned with becoming truly free or independent by means of ongoing training—the practice of endurance by reducing desires and cultivating self-control; the active embrace of hardship and suffering; the pursuit of a shameless, self-sufficient, and simple or frugal life centered on necessity alone. Accordingly, Cynics wore a simple outfit consisting of long hair and a beard, a worn garment, a staff, and a leather bag that held everything they required for their spare existence.

The other aspect had to do with a mission to others to help them see through human vanity and the apparent value of many human conventions and cherished things in order to live a freer and more authentic and virtuous life according to nature. Frank truth-telling in the context of conversation or street preaching was the central way that Cynics reached others.

For nearly a millennium, from the late fifth century BC to the late fifth century AD, the average person would have encountered Cynicism through its representatives who lived and begged and taught in the open air. There they would be in the typical Cynic outfit, walking along the road, or standing in the marketplace, or sitting by a temple taking care of their own business, or talking with others, preaching even, criticizing society and challenging everyone to wake up in order to live freer, more authentic and self-sufficient lives. It's a challenge that remains open to us today.

So let's go! Let's listen to what the Cynics have to say. Their wisdom. Their way. But more, let's practice—let's do, let's be, let's live. And let's share.

As for your approach to what follows, feel free to skip around or go through it consecutively, page after page. You'll find that some selections will captivate you while others won't—at least at first glance.

Whatever you do, carry *The Wisdom and Way of the Cynics* in your pocket, and return to it again and again.

---

*Note: though modified, this brief introduction is a portion of the introduction to the Cynics and Cynicism that appears in the Cave's *The Best of the Cynics: The Lives, Writings & Teachings of the Ancient Cynics*.

SOURCES & ABBREVIATIONS
FOR *THE WISDOM & WAY OF THE CYNICS*

Most of the selections (quotations) included in *The Wisdom & Way of the Cynics: Pocket Edition* come from the Cave's *The Best of the Cynics: The Lives, Writings & Teachings of the Ancient Cynics*. That said, they are occasionally slightly modified to better fit the format and purpose of this book.

Though always offering the philosophy (the ideas, sayings, practices, and the like) of the Cynics, the selections originally came from the following ancient authors and works. The **bolded** abbreviations (for example, **T** for Teles of Megara or **DL** for Diogenes Laertius) let you know who said what.

• Diogenes Laertius (**DL**), *Lives and Opinions of Eminent Philosophers*. Diogenes was a third century AD biographer, who focused on the philosophers, from the origins of philosophy to Epicurus. DL itself will indicate a saying or anecdote and the like recorded by Diogenes Laertius. By contrast, when you see **ADL**, **DDL**, **CDL**, or **MDL**, know that these are, respectively, sayings of, or they contain quotations of, the Cynics Antisthenes (c. 445-c. 365 BC), Diogenes of Sinope (c. 410-c. 323 BC), Crates of Thebes (c. 365-c. 285 BC), or Metrocles of Maroneia (fourth century BC) recorded by Diogenes Laertius in his *Lives*.

• **AX** signifies Antisthenes (c. 445-c. 365 BC) speaking in Xenophon's *Symposium*. Xenophon (c. 430-354 BC) was an Athenian soldier, statesman, and historian.

• **T** points to Teles of Megara, the third century BC author of *discourses* covering such topics as self-sufficiency, exile, poverty and wealth, and pleasure.

- **LD** and **LC** indicate the *letters* of Diogenes of Sinope and Crates of Thebes, respectively. Though they are not genuine, they are clearly Cynic insofar as they remain faithful to Cynic themes.
- **DC** is either Diogenes of Sinope in Dio Chrysostom's *orations*, or Dio Chrysostom himself. Dio Chrysostom (c. 40-c. 112 AD) was a rhetorician and a sometimes practicing Cynic.
- **EP** is the Stoic Epictetus (c. 55-135 AD), who authored many *discourses*, one expounding the true nature of the Cynic life.
- **AP** refers to Apuleius (second century AD), who wrote about the Cynic Crates of Thebes (c. 365-c. 285 BC) in his *Florida*.
- **LS** indicates the Cynic (unnamed) in Lucian of Samosata's dialogue, *The Cynic*. Lucian was born c. 120 AD.
- **J** points to Julian, the third century AD Roman philosopher-emperor, who wrote two *orations* touching on Cynicism.
- **B** is Basil (the Great) of Caesarea (c. 329-379 AD). Though he was not a Cynic, he admired the Cynics and was clearly influenced by them, as we see in his *letters* and other writings.
- **OTHER AUTHORS** are individually identified.

The following selections present a few **examples** of how the source or author abbreviations work:

> Virtue is a weapon that cannot be taken away—ADL (a saying of Antisthenes found in Diogenes Laertius' *Lives*).
>
> Take care of your soul—but your body only so far as what is necessary—LC (from one of Crates of Thebes' letters).

TOPICS *with* SELECTIONS

Part 1

THE CYNIC WAY OF LIFE

"Let him who wishes to be a Cynic philosopher *realize that* . . . reason and a certain plan of life . . . are the marks of the Cynic philosophy."
—Julian the Roman emperor

1

DOING PHILOSOPHY

1. Do philosophy more often than you breathe. I say this because living well, which philosophy produces, is more choiceworthy than simply living, which breathing produces. —LC

2. Don't do philosophy as others have done it, but as Antisthenes first practiced it, that which Diogenes brought to fulfillment. But if doing philosophy in this manner is troublesome or difficult, at least it is short. One must go for happiness, as Diogenes used to say, even if the going is through fire. —LC

3. To the one who said, "I am unfit for doing philosophy," Diogenes replied, "Why then do you live if you do not care to live happily?" —DDL

4. If I aspire to wisdom, this is being a philosopher. —DDL

5. It was because of my exile that I began to pursue philosophy. —DDL

6. Diogenes had an amazing gift of persuasion. He

could easily conquer anyone with words. It is said that a certain man from Aegina named Onesicritus sent Androsthenes, one of his two sons, to Athens. And when he listened to Diogenes, he stayed there. Eventually, the father sent his older son, Philiscus, to Athens in order to search for Androsthenes. But he was kept there in the same way. Finally, when the father himself arrived, he was equally attracted to the pursuit of philosophy, just as his sons were. And so he joined his sons—so magical was the charm in Diogenes' words.—DL

7. We should study philosophy until generals appear the same as donkey-drivers.—CDL

8. When he was asked what result he obtained from philosophy, Antisthenes said, "The ability to be in my own company and to be acquainted with myself."—ADL

9. When Diogenes once saw a young man studying philosophy, he said, "Well done, inasmuch as you are leading those who admire bodily things to the beauty of the soul."—DDL

10. When someone asked him what sort of learning is the most necessary, Antisthenes said, "The learning that strips away anything that must be unlearned."—ADL

1 ▪ Doing Philosophy

11. Law is a fine thing, but it is not better than philosophy. I say this because law forces a man to do no wrong, whereas philosophy instructs him. —LC

12. Demetrius of Magnesia tells a story that Crates deposited his money with a banker, making the following agreement with him. If his sons became ordinary people, then he was to give the money to them. But if they became philosophers, then he was to apportion it among the people, since his sons would need nothing if they were philosophers. —DL

13. When asked "what he gained from philosophy," Crates answered, "A measure of lupin beans and no one to worry about." —CDL

14. In response to the man who asked, "What will it mean for me to do philosophy?" Crates said, "You will easily be able to open your bag and freely give from it rather than, as now, writhing and irresolute and shaking as men do with disabled hands.... If you notice that your bag is empty, you will not suffer distress.... You will live satisfied with what you have, neither desiring what is absent nor being displeased with whatever comes your way." —T

15. Rid yourself of every passion by means of holy

philosophy.—LD

16. To Rhesus, greetings: Phrynichus the Larissaean, a student of mine, longs to see Argos, "where horses graze." He will not need much from you since he is a philosopher.—LD

17. To Hipparchia: I admire you for your yearning—that, even though you are a woman, you reached out for philosophy and have become a member of our school, which has terrified even men by its severity. Be earnest to bring to completion what you have begun. You will do so, I know well, if you do not let Crates, your husband, leave you behind.—LD

18. To Hipparchia: Return with speed. You can still catch Diogenes while he is living—for he is already near the end of his life. Return, then, so that you can take leave of him with an embrace and come to know what philosophy may do in the most fearful circumstances.—LC

2

THE CYNIC WAY OF LIFE

1. The Cynic school is a way of life. —DL

2. Antisthenes used to walk about five miles to Athens every day in order to hear Socrates. He learned the art of endurance from him, imitating his indifference to suffering. So it was that he began the Cynic philosophy and the Cynic way of life. —DL

3. When someone said that life is bad, Diogenes said, "Not life, but living badly." —DDL

4. The Cynics were pleased to strip philosophy of logic and the study of nature in order to devote themselves solely to ethics. —DL

5. I still believe that, even before Heracles, not only among the Greeks but among the non-Greeks also, there were men who practiced this philosophy. For it seems to be in some ways a common or universal philosophy, and the most natural, and to demand no special study whatsoever. But it is enough simply to choose the excellent by longing for virtue and fleeing from vice. And so there is no need to turn over

countless books. For, as the saying goes, "Much learning does not teach understanding." Nor is it necessary to subject oneself to any part of such a discipline as they must undergo who enter other schools of philosophy. —J

6. Long is the path that leads to happiness through words alone. But the path that leads to happiness through the practice of daily deeds is short. —LC

7. I came, Father, to Athens, and learning that Socrates' associate was teaching about happiness, I went to him. And he happened to be speaking about the paths that lead to happiness. He declared that there are two and not many paths—and that one is a shortcut and the other is long. . . . I, superior to the hardships, chose the steep and troublesome path—for the man speeding on to happiness must go on even if it is through fire and sword. —LD

8. The Cynics hold that the goal of life is to live according to virtue. —DL

9. Whenever they hear about a shortcut leading to happiness, the many throw themselves at it just as we do with philosophy. But when they reach the path and see how difficult it is, they retreat, going backward, as if

weak or sick. And rather than complaining about their own softness, they find fault with our freedom from passion and suffering. —LD

10. You find fault with my life for how hard and toilsome it is, and that no one will practice it because it is so difficult and harsh. But I have increased its difficulty on purpose so that those who imitate me might know not to enjoy fine things. —LD

11. Diogenes used to say that he imitated the chorus masters. They also set the note a little high so that the rest would hit the right note. —DL

12. Cynicism is a shortcut upon the path of virtue. —DL

13. One must go for happiness, as Diogenes used to say, even if the going is through fire. —LC

14. Hipparchia, the sister of Metrocles, was also captured by the teachings of the Cynics. They were both from Maroneia. Hipparchia fell in love with the teachings and life of Crates—so much so that she would not pay attention to any of her suitors, nor to their wealth, nor to their nobility of birth, nor to their beauty. No, Crates was everything to her. She would even threaten her parents with suicide if she were not

given in marriage to him. Accordingly, they called on Crates to talk her out of it. He did all he could. But when he failed to persuade her, he got up, took off his clothes right in front of her, and said, "This is the man you hope to marry. Here are his possessions. Deliberate and make your choice with these facts in mind since you will not be my partner unless you share in my pursuits." The girl made her choice. She adopted his manner of dressing and went around with him as her husband. —DL

15. *We are called Cynics not because we are* indifferent *to things but* because we doggedly stick with things that are unbearable to others on account of softness and mere opinions. . . . Stand your ground, therefore, and practice Cynicism with me. —LC

16. The man who is beginning to be a Cynic should first censure himself severely and cross-examine himself, and without any self-flattery ask himself the following questions in precise terms: whether he enjoys lavish and expensive food; whether he cannot do without a soft bed; whether he is the slave of honor and reputation; whether it is his ambition to get people to look at and admire him; and, even though it is empty, he still judges it an honor. —J

17. Let the man who wishes to be a Cynic philosopher not merely adopt their tattered cloak or leather bag or staff or their way of wearing the hair, as though he were like a man walking unshaved and illiterate in a village that lacked barbershops and schools, but let him consider that reason rather than a staff, and a certain plan of life rather than a leather bag, are the marks of the Cynic philosophy.—J

18. The better sort of Cynics assert that in addition to the other good things bestowed on us by mighty Heracles, it was he who gave to mankind the greatest example of the Cynic way of life.—J

3

THE CYNIC OUTFIT

1. Cynics teach that men should live simply, procuring for themselves only necessary food and wearing only one piece of clothing, a worn garment. . . . Diogenes used to say that it was characteristic of the gods to need nothing, and that, consequently, when a man desires very little or nothing at all, he is like the gods. —DL

2. *Lycinus:* Give an account of yourself, my man. You wear a beard and let your hair grow. You eschew shirts, exhibit your skin, and your feet are bare. You choose a wandering, outcast, beastly life. Unlike other people, you make your own body the object of your severities. You go from place to place sleeping on the hard ground where chance finds you, with the result that your old cloak, neither light nor soft nor anything to look at to begin with, is loaded down with filth. Why?

The Cynic: It meets my needs. It was easy to come by, and it gives its owner no trouble. It is sufficient for me. Tell me, do you not call extravagance a vice?

Lycinus: Oh, yes.

The Cynic: And frugality a virtue?

Lycinus: Yes, again.

The Cynic: Then if you find me living frugally, and others extravagantly, why blame me instead of them?—LS

3. Our Cynic aspirations are considerably different from those of other people. We want less rather than desiring more and more. It is no wonder that our outfit is different since the peculiarity of our underlying principle is so different.—LS

4. I cannot understand why you allow a harpist his proper attire, as well as the fluteplayer and tragic actor, but you will not be consistent and recognize an outfit or uniform for a good man. . . . If good men are to have a uniform of their own, there can be none better than that which a licentious man will consider most improper and will decisively reject for himself.—LS

5. My uniform consists of a rough hairy skin, a threadbare cloak, long hair, and bare feet.—LS

6. The tattered cloak, the shaggy hair, the whole outfit that you ridicule has the effect that it enables me to live a quiet life, doing what I want and keeping the company I wish to keep. No ignorant,

uneducated person will have anything to say to one dressed like this. And the ones who live softly turn the other way as soon as I come into view. But refined and reasonable men approach me, those who long for virtue. These are attached to me most of all since I delight in these kinds of men. I don't hang out at the doors of the so-called happy men. Rather, I judge their gold crowns and purple vanity and laugh at these men. —LS

7. You spit on my tattered cloak and leather bag as though they were burdensome and difficult for me, and on my life as though it were useless, doing no good. . . . As for me, I pursued these things with virtue. What greater proof can I offer than not changing my course toward a life of pleasure and luxury, even though I could have? . . . What enemy would march against one who is self-sufficient and simple? . . . In conformity with this, the soul has been purified of vice and has been released from empty opinion. It has cast out immoderate desires and has been taught to speak the truth and to show contempt for other false things. —LD

8. Antisthenes wore only one garment. He was the first to fold or double over his cloak, which was rather threadbare. He carried a staff and a leather bag. —DL

9. Diodorus of Aspendos . . . let his beard grow long and used a staff and leather bag. —DL

10. Heracles roved all over Europe and Asia, even though he did not look at all like any of these athletes. For where could he have advanced, had he carried so much flesh, or required so much meat or drink, or fell into such depths of sleep? No, he was alert and lean like a lion, with sharp eyes and sensitive ears. He didn't worry about when it was hot or cold, and he had no use for a bed, or a shawl, or a rug. He was clad in a dirty skin, with an air of hunger about him, as he helped the good and punished the bad. —DC

11. To the man who was proud of wearing a lion's skin, the words of Diogenes of Sinope were, "Stop dishonoring virtue's clothing." —DL

12. *Like Heracles (Hercules),* Crates went half-naked and was distinguished by the club he carried. He sprang from that same Thebes where men say that Hercules was born. . . . Before he became Crates pure and simple, he was accounted one of the chief men in Thebes. . . . His lands were rich and his clothing sumptuous. —AP

13. As for my clothing, Homer writes that Odysseus, the wisest man among the Greeks, wore the same

when he returned home from Ilium with the counsel of Athena. . . . The outfit is so beautiful that men together agree that it was not a discovery of men but of the gods. *Homer wrote that* "Athena threw around him a tattered covering, an ugly tunic, filthy and torn and full of stale smoke. And about him she cast a swift deer's big hide, all stripped of its hair. And she gave him a staff, and a shameful leather pouch, all full of holes, hanging from him by a strap made of twisted rope."—LD

14. I have begun to see myself as the hero Agamemnon. My staff is his scepter. My doubled-over cloak is his military cloak. And my leather bag is his shield.—LD

15. Bread and water, a bed of straw, and a tattered cloak teach moderation and patient endurance.—LD

16. Do not grieve my friend, Olympias, with the fact that I wear a tattered cloak and go about begging among human beings. For this is nothing shameful, as you say, nor is it anything to look down on relative to free men. Rather, it is noble and can serve as weaponry against the appearances and opinions that battle against life. It was not from Antisthenes that I first learned these lessons. No, it was from the gods and heroes and those men who turned Greece toward wisdom—men such as Homer and the tragic poets.—LD

17. To live as a Cynic is not what it seems. You say, "I wear a cloak now and I will wear it then. I sleep on a hard surface now and I will sleep on a hard one then. I will take in addition a little bag now and a staff, and I will go around and begin to beg and to abuse those whom I meet. And if I see any man plucking the hair out of his body, I will rebuke him—or if he has dressed his hair in some fancy manner, or if he struts around in purple." If you imagine that being a Cynic is something like this, *a matter of clothing and the like,* then stay far away from it. Do not come near to it—it is not at all for you.—EP

18. The clothing does not produce a Cynic; rather, the Cynic the clothing.—LC

Part 2

CYNIC GOALS

"The object and goal of the Cynic philosophy, as with every philosophy, is to be happy—but to be happy in a life lived according to nature."
—Julian the Roman emperor

"The Cynics hold that the goal of life is to live according to virtue."
—Diogenes Laertius

4

THE GOAL OF LIFE

1. Do well. —LD

2. The main goal of *the* Cynics . . . is how they themselves might be happy. —J

3. The Cynics hold that the goal of life is to live according to virtue. . . . Therefore, some have said that Cynicism is a shortcut upon the path of virtue. —DL

4. The goal of Cynicism is to live according to virtue, in the manner of Diogenes of Sinope and Zeno of Citium. —SUDA

6. Now the object and goal of the Cynic philosophy, as with every philosophy, is to be happy—but to be happy in a life lived according to nature and not according to the opinions of the many. Plants also do well, and indeed all animals also, whenever each one, without hindrance, reaches the goal that follows from and is in accord with nature. But even among the gods, this is the definition of happiness—that their state should be according to their nature, and that they should be independent. —J

7. Cynics teach that men should live simply, procuring for themselves only necessary food and wearing only one piece of clothing, a worn garment. They think very little of wealth and reputation and noble birth. Some Cynics get by on herbs and vegetables and cold water. They live in any kind of shelter, or even large wine-jars, just as did Diogenes, who used to say that it was characteristic of the gods to need nothing, and that, consequently, when a man desires very little or nothing at all, he is like the gods. —DL

8. The following line tells us what Crates of Thebes gained from philosophy: "A measure of lupin beans and no one to worry about." —DL

9. Pleasure is not the goal of life. —T

5

HAPPINESS

1. The main goal of the Cynics. . . . was how they themselves might be happy. —J

2. We Cynics say that the good and excellent man, and no other man, is called happy. —LC

3. I came, father, to Athens, and learning that Socrates' associate was teaching about happiness, I went to him. And he happened to be speaking about the paths that lead to happiness. He declared that there are two and not many paths—and that one is a shortcut and the other is long. . . . The one is short, steep, and troublesome; the other is long, smooth, and easy. . . . While the others, who were struck with fear at the troublesome and steep nature of the one path, called on him to lead them along the long and smooth one, I, superior to the hardships, chose the steep and troublesome path—for the man speeding on to happiness must go on even if it is through fire and sword. —LD

4. One must go for happiness, as Diogenes used to say, even if the going is through fire. —LC

5. I do not see how someone will live a happy life if he really must measure it by an excess of pleasure. —T

6. When someone asked him what the greatest happiness was among human beings, Antisthenes said, "To die happy." —ADL

7. Where are you hurrying? What are you doing, you miserable men? Like blind people you are wandering up and down. You are going by another road and have left the true road. You search for prosperity and happiness where they are not. —EP

8. Why do you seek happiness outside yourself? In the body? It is not there. . . . It is not in possessions. . . . It is not in power. —EP

9. Most of the precious instruments of happiness that you so pride yourselves on are won only with unhappiness and hardships. Give a moment's thought, if you will, to the gold you all pray for, to the silver, the costly houses, the elaborate clothing. And do not forget all the trouble and toil and danger they cost — the blood and death and ruin. Not only do large numbers of men perish at sea on their account, but many endure miseries in producing them. Moreover, they're very likely to be fought for — the desire for them

makes friends plot against friends, children against parents, wives against husbands. —LS

10. How is there a road to happiness where there are perturbations, griefs, fears, unsatisfied desires, unavoidable aversions for things, envies and jealousies? —EP

11. The happy man will also be free from passion and trouble. But whoever is in distress and pain and fear—how could such a one be satisfied with life? And if not satisfied, how could such a one be happy? Or if pain touches him, how could fear and anguish and anger and pity not do so? For when these things exist, human beings feel pain and distress. —T

12. Take care of your soul—but your body only so far as what is necessary, and externals not even that much. I say this because happiness is not a pleasure that requires external things. —LC

13. If the happy life must be measured by the yardstick of excessive pleasure, then no one, says Crates, will be judged happy. —T

14. Long is the path that leads to happiness through words alone. But the path that leads to happiness through the practice of daily deeds is short. —LC

15. We must say that happiness resides in our minds, in the best and noblest part of us. —J

16. The noble and excellent man believes that his hardships are his greatest opponents, and always wants to battle with them day and night—not to win a sprig of parsley, as so many goats might do, nor for a bit of wild olive, or of pine, but to win happiness and virtue throughout all the days of his life—DC

17. And coming to the place where Happiness exists, I said, "Because of you, Happiness, and the greater good, I persisted in drinking water and eating cardamom and sleeping on the ground." Responding to me, Happiness said, "But rather than a hardship, I will make these things sweeter to you than the goods of wealth that human beings honor before me." . . . And from that point on, when I listened to Happiness talking about this, I no longer ate or drank these things as a matter of practice, but as a pleasure. —LD

18. Diogenes lived more happily than one who is counted the happiest of men. And he actually used to assert that he lived more happily than such a man. But if you do not believe me, try his way of life not by talking about it but by doing it. Then you'll get it. —J

6

VIRTUE & VICE

1. The Cynics hold that the goal of life is to live according to virtue. —DL

2. Some have said that Cynicism is a shortcut upon the path of virtue. —DL

3. The Cynic will only be able to do those things that are done according to virtue. —LD

4. Diogenes was courageous in his practice of virtue. —LC

5. I still believe that, even before Heracles, not only among the Greeks but among the non-Greeks also, there were men who practiced this philosophy. For it seems to be in some ways a common or universal philosophy, and the most natural, and to demand no special study whatsoever. But it is enough simply to choose the excellent by longing for virtue and fleeing from vice. —J

6. Virtue is sufficient for happiness. Virtue requires nothing more than the strength of Socrates. —ADL

7. We Cynics say that the good and excellent man,

and no other man, is called happy. —LC

8. Those who wish to be immortal must live piously and justly. —ADL

9. Good men are images of the gods. —DDL

10. The well-born and the virtuous are one and the same. —ADL

11. To the man who was proud of wearing a lion's skin, Diogenes' words were, "Stop dishonoring virtue's clothing." —DDL

12. Virtue is the same for a woman as it is for a man. —ADL

13. The most beautiful adornment is the one that adorns you most beautifully. But the one that adorns you most beautifully is the one that produces a well-ordered, regular, moderate life. It is this adornment that produces this well-ordered life. It seems to me that both Penelope and Alcestis adorned themselves in this manner. Even now they are hymned and honored for their virtue. So that you might be a match for their kind, then, try to cling to this advice. —LC

14. Virtue enters the soul by means of training—not automatically as happens with vice.—LC

15. Diogenes declared that there are two kinds of exercise—training of the soul and training of the body. And that the latter exercise gives rise to perceptions that facilitate virtuous deeds. Each practice is incomplete and ineffectual without the other. . . . He offered positive proof for how easily we arrive at virtue by means of physical exercise. One can see that craftsmen acquire hand-speed with careful practice. And flute players and athletes excel by means of their own labor. And if these transferred the practices to the soul, then the exercises would not be without profit and incomplete.—DL

16. The Cynics hold that virtue can be taught. . . . Once it is acquired it cannot be lost.—DL

17. When asked what a man must do to be noble and good, Antisthenes said, "You must learn from those who know well that your vices must be rejected."—ADL

18. Virtue is a weapon that cannot be taken away.—ADL

19. Antisthenes held that virtue is something you do—it is a matter of deeds. It doesn't require a stockpile of

arguments or much learning. —DL

20. To Epimenides, greetings: You stay at home delighting your belly and adorning your body instead of enduring by means of virtue. I hear that you profess virtue—and such an act did not seem incredible to me, for, according to Simonides, it is difficult to be good but easy to profess goodness. —LD

21. Virtue alone is that by which the soul can be strengthened and delivered from its afflictions. —LD

22. Men strive in punching and kicking to outdo one another, but no one strives to become a good and noble man. —DDL

23. It doesn't seem to me that everyone is capable of living virtuously as we understand it. —LD

24. All slaves are enslaved either through the law or by means of vice. —LC

25. Indigestion is caused by gluttony and vice. —LC

26. The Cynics teach that whatever is between virtue and vice should be counted as indifferent, that is, neither good nor bad. —DL

27. City-states are destroyed when they are unable to judge the difference between good and bad men. —ADL

28. "It is odd," Antisthenes said, "that we weed out certain grasses from the grain and the unfit in war, but we do not excuse worthless men from the business of the city-state." —ADL

29. To Charmides, greetings: Your acquaintance Euremus offered me many sophisms and dark sayings . . . But I don't think virtue is exalted by this sort of speech. —LD

7

FOLLOWING NATURE

1. Cynicism, as you know, is an inspection of nature. —LD

2. Nature is mighty. It is this that we restore as the deliverance and preservation of humankind, since nature has been tossed from life thanks to the influence of opinion and appearance. —LD

3. I am heaven's dog . . . living according to nature, free under Zeus. —LD

4. Diogenes the Cynic asserted that he could counter . . . convention with nature. —DL

5. It was evident that Diogenes acted according to what he said—altering the currency, as it were, or reevaluating human customs, granting nothing at all in this way to human custom and law, but following nature. —DL

6. Rather than unprofitable, toilsome exercises, men should prefer those which follow nature in order to live happily. —DDL

7. I pray that . . . I might need bedding no more than the lion, and costly food no more than the dog. Let my sufficient bed be the whole earth, my house this cosmos, and my chosen food the easiest to get. —LS

8. To Apolexis, greetings: I spoke with you about a place to live. Thank you for taking this on. But when I beheld a snail, I found a house that would keep off the wind—that is, the wine jar in the Mētrōon. So then I release you from this service. Let us rejoice over this discovery of nature. —LD

9. I do not have the smallest admiration for the present generation's wonderful felicity—tables! clothes! bodies artificially polished all over! no hair growing in any of the places where nature plants it! —LS

10. *A brief description of the Cynic:* You honor nature. You abstain from all sorts of good things, utilizing them no more than the beasts. Your drink is water, just like theirs. You eat what you pick up, like a dog. And the dog's bed is as good as yours—straw is enough for either of you. Then your clothes are no more presentable than a beggar's. You refrain from all the wonderful paraphernalia of civilization. —LS

11. We Cynics live as we were born. —LD

12. That part of you, whatever it is, has been neglected by you and is corrupted—the part by which we desire and avoid, move toward and turn away from things. How has it been neglected? He does not know the essence of the good for which he is made by nature and the essence of the bad. Nor does he know what is his own and what belongs to another.—EP

13. Once when Diogenes saw a young man behaving effeminately, he said, "Are you not ashamed that the plans you have for yourself are worse than what nature has for you? For nature made you a man and you are forcing yourself to be a woman."—DL

8

FREEDOM

1. Diogenes declared that his manner of life was the same as that of Heracles. He preferred freedom more than everything else. —DL

2. I am heaven's dog ... living according to nature, free under Zeus. —LD

3. Diogenes: "I've learned that you carried all your property to the assembly and handed it over to your fatherland. And standing in the middle of everyone as a herald would, you proclaimed, 'Crates, the son of Crates, sets Crates free.'" —LD

4. The Cynic should not wish to hide anything that he does. And if he does, he is gone—he has lost the character of a Cynic, of a man who lives under the open sky, of a free man. He has begun to fear some external thing. He has begun to require concealment. —EP

5. The old cloak, the shaggy hair, the whole outfit that you ridicule has the effect that it enables me to live a quiet life, doing what I want and keeping the company I wish to keep. —LS

6. Plato saw Diogenes washing greens. So he approached him and quietly said to him, "If you had paid court to the tyrant Dionysus, you would not now be washing vegetables." Equally quiet, Diogenes replied, "If you had washed vegetables, you wouldn't have paid court to the tyrant Dionysus." —DDL

7. And how is it possible that a man who has nothing—who is naked, houseless, and without a hearth, who is squalid, without a slave or a city—how can such a man pass a life that flows well? Behold, God has sent you a man to show you that it is possible: "Look at me," the Cynic says, "I who am without a city, without a house, without possessions, without a slave. I sleep on the ground. I have no wife, no children, no praetorium; rather, I have only the earth and the heavens, and one poor cloak. And what do I want? Am I not without pain and sorrow? Without fear? Am I not free? . . . Who, when he sees me, does not think that he sees his king and master?" —EP

8. The Cynic must not only, by showing the qualities of the soul, prove to the average person that it is in his power, independent of the things which they admire, to be a good man, but he must also show by his body that his simple and frugal way of living in the open air does not injure even the body. —EP

9. Let others sleep with their pleasures as they are eager to do! For if they live this kind of life, then even greater hardship will befall them than those by which they slander us. And so they are shamefully enslaved in every circumstance. —LD

10. Well then, do you possess *nothing* that is free? "Perhaps nothing." And who is able to compel you to assent to that which appears false? "No man." And who can compel you *not* to assent to that which appears true? "No man." By this, then, you see that there is something in you that is naturally free. —EP

11. But to desire or to be averse from, or to move toward or away from an object, or to prepare yourself or to propose to do anything—which of you can do any of these things unless he has received an impression of that which is profitable or that which is the fitting thing to do? "No man." You also have in these things, then, something that is unhindered and free. Wretched men, work this out, take care of this, seek for good here. —EP

12. Whenever they hear about a shortcut leading to happiness, the many throw themselves at it just as we do with philosophy. But when they reach the path and see how difficult it is, they retreat, going

backward, as if weak or sick. And rather than complaining about their own softness, they find fault with our freedom from passion and suffering. —LD

9

REPUTATION & OPINION

1. A bad reputation is a good thing. —ADL

2. Do not be distressed, father, that I call myself a dog. . . . Instead, be delighted that your son is content with little and that he is free from popular opinion, to which everyone, both the Greeks and barbarians, are enslaved. —LD

3. When Antisthenes was applauded by bad men, he said, "I'm afraid that I have done something wrong." —ADL

4. One man said to Antisthenes, "The many praise you." In response, he said, "Why? What wrong have I done?" —ADL

5. Pay attention to your enemies, for they are the first to notice your faults. —ADL

6. When Antisthenes was told that Plato was abusing him, he said, "It is a royal privilege to do what is noble and to hear bad things said about what I do." —ADL

7. When men are slandered, they should bear with it more courageously than if they were pelted with stones. —ADL

8. Diogenes thought that he should fight stubbornly and war against opinion as much as against wild beasts and wicked men. —DC

9. As long as you are a slave to the opinions of the many, you have not yet approached freedom or tasted its nectar. —J

10. The Cynic must use the respect that he has built up and gained for himself as his protection. —EP

11. The Cynic should not wish to hide anything that he does. And if he does, he is gone—he has lost the character of a Cynic, of a man who lives under the open sky, of a free man. He has begun to fear some external thing. He has begun to require concealment. —EP

12. Diogenes used to call demagogues the servants of the crowd and the wreathes crowning them the flowering of popularity. —DL

13. Diogenes used to call all rhetoricians and those who spoke for fame "three times human," by which

he meant, "three times wretched." —DL

14. Diogenes called an ignorant rich man "a sheep with golden wool." —DL

15. I don't hang out at the doors of the so-called happy men. Rather, I judge their gold crowns and purple vanity and laugh at these men. —LS

16. Diogenes ridiculed noble birth and reputation and all such distinctions, calling them the showy ornaments of vice. —DL

17. One day Alexander the Great stood by Diogenes and said, "I am Alexander, the great and mighty king." In response, Diogenes said, "And I am Diogenes, the dog." —DL

18. To the Sinopians: It is far better to be disparaged by you Sinopians than to be praised by you. —LD

19. To Metrocles: Don't turn back even if, because of this Cynic way of life, people call you a dog or some other worse name. —LD

20. Monimus thought very little of reputation and was eager for the truth. —DL

21. To Perdiccas: If you are presently fighting against opinions and appearances, enemies which, I say, are stronger and harm you more than both the Thracians and Paeonians, and if you are working to subdue the human passions, then send for me. I say this because I am able to battle against these as a general does. —LD

23. If you become someone who looks down on pleasure, and someone who doesn't set himself against hard work, and someone who considers equal both good and bad reputation, and someone who doesn't fear death, then it will be possible for you to do whatever you wish without suffering distress. —T

Actuality versus Appearance

1. Being good is better than appearing good. —T

2. Living well is better than not living well. —T

3. Diogenes of Sinope would generally chide men for the way they prayed, declaring that they asked for the seemingly good rather than the truly good. —DL

4. Some people say that appearing to be just is better than actually being just. And yet appearing to be good is not better than actually being good—is it?
   Of course not.
   Tell me, then, do men play their parts well because they appear to be good actors or because they actually are good?
   Because they actually are.
   And do men play the lyre well because they appear to be good lyre players or because they actually are good?
   Because they actually are.
   And, generally, do men do well in all other things because they appear to be good or because they actually are good?

Because they actually are.
Accordingly, living well is better than not living well. Being good, then, is better than appearing good, for the just man is good—not the man who appears just.—T

5. What about the other things that human beings imagine goods? Would you rather . . . possess them or appear to possess them? For instance, would you prefer to see or to appear to see? To be healthy or to appear so? To be strong or to appear so? To be well-off and have friends or to appear so? Again, regarding the goods of the soul, would you prefer to understand and be wise or to appear so? To be without pain and sorrow or to appear so? To be confident, to be without fear, to be courageous or to appear so? Yet when it comes to justice, would you rather appear to be just rather than actually being just?—T

6. You say, I would rather appear to be courageous than to actually be courageous.

But is not the courageous man also the one who is actually fearless and free from any pain and grief? Why do you wish to appear courageous?

Because people will honor me.

They will! But they will also position you as the right-hand man in battle. And they will call on you to engage in single combat.... Then what do you imagine will happen since you are actually a coward and in danger? —T

7. You pretend and hide the truth just like politicians do. —T

8. We should not profess and promise much and then practice what is not sufficient. Rather, we should demonstrate that our lives correspond with our words. This is what I attempt to do in my own case—what I hope to be a witness of. *And I am not only thinking of others.* I am speaking of my own soul, whose notice I cannot escape when I miss the mark. —LD

9. To Epimenides, greetings: You stay at home delighting your belly and adorning your body instead of enduring by means of virtue. I hear that you profess virtue—and such an act did not seem incredible to me, for, according to Simonides, it is difficult to be good but easy to profess goodness. —LD

11

REAL HUMAN BEINGS

1. Diogenes lit a lamp in the middle of the day and walked around saying, "I'm searching for a human being." —DDL

2. When he was leaving the public baths, someone asked whether there were many human beings bathing. Diogenes said, "No." Yet when another man asked him whether there was a great crowd of bathers, he said, "Yes." —DL

3. When he was returning from Olympia, someone asked him whether there was a large crowd. "Yes," he replied, "there was a great crowd, but very few human beings." —DL

4. Someone said to him, "I conquered men at the Pythian games." Diogenes responded, "In fact, I conquer men. You merely conquer slaves." —DL

5. At Olympia, the herald announced, "Dioxippus is victorious over men!" Diogenes said, "More exactly, he is victorious over slaves—I over men." —DL

6. "Tell me, who are your competitors?" a man asked. "Hardships," Diogenes replied, "that are very severe and impossible to overcome for gluttonous and folly-stricken men who feast all day long and snore at night, but which yield to thin, spare men, whose waists are more pinched in than those of wasps." —DC

7. When a couple was sacrificing to the gods so that a son might be born to them, Diogenes said, "Why don't you sacrifice to ensure what kind of man your son will be?" —DDL

12

HEROIC EXAMPLES

1. The better sort of Cynics assert that in addition to the other good things bestowed on us by mighty Heracles, it was he who gave to mankind the greatest example of the Cynic way of life.—J

2. Heracles thought that he should fight stubbornly and war against opinion as much as against wild beasts and wicked men.—DC

3. Antisthenes argued that hard work, with all its toil and suffering, is something good. He did so by pointing to the examples of great Heracles and Cyrus.—DL

4. Take Heracles, the best man that ever lived, a divine man, and rightly considered a god. Was it unhappiness that made him go around in nothing but a lion's skin, insensible to all the needs you feel? No, he was not unhappy, the man who relieved the misfortunes of others. He was not poor, he who ruled land and sea. Wherever he went, he was master. He never met his superior or his equal as long as he lived. Do you suppose, then, that he could not get coverings or clothes or shoes, and that's why he went around as he did? We

cannot draw this conclusion. Rather, he possessed self-control and was able to endure. He wanted to be powerful, strong. He didn't want luxury. —LS

5. Heracles' disciple Theseus was the best of his generation. He too chose to go without shoes and to be naked. He was content to let his hair and beard grow. He was not the only one; rather, all those of old who lived when he lived were satisfied in this way. —LS

6. The poets tell that Hercules of old by his valor subdued all the wild monsters of legend, beast or man, and purged all the world of them. Even so our philosopher Crates was truly a Hercules in the conquest of anger, envy, avarice, lust, and all the other monstrous and shameful things that plague the human soul. He expelled all these pests from their minds, purged households, and tamed vice. —AP

7. To Mnasos: Do not abstain from the most beautiful adornment, but adorn yourself each day so that you may be different from others. The most beautiful adornment is the one that adorns you most beautifully. But the one that adorns you most beautifully is the one that produces a well-ordered, regular, moderate life. It is this adornment that produces this well-ordered life. It seems to me that both Penelope and

Alcestis adorned themselves in this manner. Even now they are hymned and honored for their virtue. So that you might be a match for their kind, then, try to cling to this advice. —LC

8. Antisthenes used to benefit so much from Socrates that he counseled his own students to become fellow-students with him of Socrates. —DL

9. It is the Cynic's responsibility, then, to be able with a loud voice, if the occasion arises, and appearing on the tragic stage, to say like Socrates: "Where are you hurrying? What are you doing, you miserable men? Like blind people you are wandering up and down. You are going by another road and have left the true road. You search for prosperity and happiness where they are not." —EP

10. If you take circumstances one way, you may experience distress. Yet if you take them in the same way as Socrates, you will not suffer. —T

11. The brave and courageous man should, like Socrates, bravely endure his death. —T

12. The chief men of Cynicism were Antisthenes, Diogenes, and Crates. The goal of their lives was, I think,

to know themselves, to be aware of empty opinions, and to lay hold of truth with their whole understanding. This is so because truth—both for gods and men—is the beginning of every good thing.—J

13. Diogenes was courageous in his practice of virtue.—LC

14. When Diogenes was sold as a slave, he endured it most nobly.—DL

15. Crates and Diogenes easily carried on when they gave up arrogance and became beggars and developed the ability to make use of a cheap and simple way of life.—T

13

THE WISE & GOOD MAN

1. The wise man is self-sufficient since all the goods of others are his. — ADL

2. Diogenes argued that all things belong to the wise by arguing as follows: "All things belong to the gods. The wise are friends of the gods, and friends hold all things in common; therefore, all things belong to the wise." — DL

3. The wise man is guided in his public acts not by the established laws but by the law of virtue. — ADL

4. Nothing is strange or helpless to the wise man. — ADL

5. A good man is worthy of love. Excellent men — serious men of character — are friends. — ADL

6. Good men *are* images of the gods. — DDL

Part 3

CYNIC TRAINING & PRACTICE

"Nothing in life is successful without training, which has the power to conquer anything."
—Diogenes of Sinope

14

TRAINING & PRACTICE

1. Diogenes said that absolutely nothing in life is successful without training, which has the power to conquer anything. —DL

2. Diogenes declared that there are two kinds of exercise—training of the soul and training of the body. And that the latter exercise gives rise to perceptions that facilitate virtuous deeds. Each practice is incomplete and ineffectual without the other. —DL

3. Diogenes offered positive proof for how easily we arrive at virtue by means of physical exercise. One can see that craftsmen acquire hand-speed with careful practice. And flute players and athletes excel by means of their own labor. And if these transferred the practices to the soul, then the exercises would not be without profit and incomplete. —DL

4. Virtue enters the soul by means of training—not automatically as happens with vice. —LC

5. Metrocles divided things in the following manner: those things that are obtained with money, such as a

house, and those things that are obtained with time and care, such as an education. —DL

6. Rather than unprofitable, toilsome exercises, men should prefer those which follow nature in order to live happily. —DDL

7. Diogenes trained the sons of Xeniades in the following manner. After their other studies, he taught them to ride, to shoot with the bow, to sling stones, and to hurl javelins. Later, when in the wrestling school, he would not allow the physical trainer to train them like athletes, but only enough to keep them looking healthy and to train them in good habits. The boys used to memorize many passages from poets and prose writers and from the writings of Diogenes himself. And he would make them practice various shortcuts and approaches to make these passages easier to remember. —DL

8. Flee not only from the worst of the vices, injustice and a lack of self-control, but also what produces them, pleasure and enjoyment. . . . Pursue not only the best of goods, self-control and endurance, but also what produces them, hard work and toil. —LC

9. Train yourselves to need very little—for this is closest to god, while the opposite is farthest. —LC

10. Keep training just as you began and earnestly set yourself in equal measure against both pleasure and hardship. —LD

11. Crates would wear a cloak thick with hair during the summer and a tattered one during the winter. —DL

12. To Hipparchia: You are persuaded that working hard is the reason why one does not have to work hard. I say this because you would not have given birth without any trouble if you had not, while pregnant, continued to work hard and toil as athletes do. —LC

13. I laud you for your good sense and am delighted that you gave up your property. You grew stronger than mere opinion faster than I expected. But return quickly. I say this because you still need training in other matters. It is not safe to spend time where no one is like you. —LD

14. When you train to look down on poverty, a bad reputation, low birth, and exile, you will live blessedly and will die in a manner that is bearable. Otherwise, you will live miserably. —LD

15. Get used to eating barley cakes and drinking water. —LC

16. Get used to washing in cold water, drinking water, eating nothing that has not come to you by means of toil and sweat, wearing a tattered cloak, and spending your time on the ground. —LC

17. One must practice eating cardamom and drinking water and wearing a light, tattered cloak. —LD

18. In summertime, Diogenes used to roll in his wine-jar house over hot sand. And in wintertime, he used to hug statues of men covered with snow. He practiced endurance in every way. —DL

19. Diogenes once begged alms from a statue. When asked why he did this, he said, "To practice being rejected." —DDL

20. Diogenes was going into a theater while everyone else was going out in the opposite direction. When someone asked him why, he said, "This is what I practice doing every day of my life." —DDL

21. Crates used to revile prostitutes on purpose in order to practice getting used to the profanity they would give him in return. —DL

22. Beg for your daily bread even from the statues of

men set up in the marketplace. A practice such as this is good considering you'll happen upon men in your begging that are even more unfeeling than statues. —LD

23. Diogenes was courageous in his practice of virtue. . . . Put on his armor and carry his weapons. —LC

24. And the disturbances and confusions that attack the soul and are derived from the body—to which this envelope of ours often constrains us for its sake to pay too much attention—Diogenes did not take into account at all. Consequently, by means of this discipline the man made his body stronger, I believe, than that of any who have contended for the prize of a crown in the games. And his soul was so disposed that he was happy. And in this happiness he was a king no less—if not even more!—than the Great King, as the Greeks used to call him in those days, by which they meant the king of Persia. —J

25. As the good actor performs the prologue well, and the middle part well, and the conclusion well, so also does the good man live the first part of life well, and the middle part well, and the end well. —T

26. *A brief description of the Cynic:* You wear a beard and let your hair grow. You eschew shirts, exhibit your

skin, and your feet are bare. You choose a wandering, outcast, beastly life. Unlike other people, you make your own body the object of your severities. You go from place to place sleeping on the hard ground where chance finds you, with the result that your old cloak, neither light nor soft nor anything to look at to begin with, is loaded down with filth. —LS

27. When Hegesias asked Diogenes to lend him one of his writings, he replied, "You are a vain and thoughtless man. For in the case of figs, you would not choose painted figs but real ones, yet in this case you pass over genuine practice for what is merely written." —DDL

28. We should not profess and promise much and then practice what is not sufficient. Rather, we should demonstrate that our lives correspond with our words. This is what I attempt to do in my own case — what I hope to be a witness of. *And I am not only thinking of others.* I am speaking of my own soul, whose notice I cannot escape when I miss the mark. —LD

29. Those who express weighty sentiments without doing anything, Diogenes used to compare to a harp. For like them, the harp can neither hear nor feel. —DL

30. To Perdiccas: If you are presently fighting against

opinions and appearances, enemies which, I say, are stronger and harm you more than both the Thracians and Paeonians, and if you are working to subdue the human passions, then send for me. I say this because I am able to battle against these as a general does. —LD

31. Long is the path that leads to happiness through words alone. But the path that leads to happiness through the practice of daily deeds is short. —LC

Soul-Care & Self-Reflection

1. Know yourself—for in doing this you would do well. If there is some sickness such as folly in your soul, then grab a doctor for it—LD

2. Take care of your soul—but your body only so far as what is necessary, and externals not even that much. I say this because happiness is not a pleasure that requires external things, nor does perfect virtue require these.—LC

3. When he was asked what result he obtained from philosophy, Antisthenes said, "The ability to be in my own company and to be acquainted with myself."—ADL

4. The Cynic Diogenes also gave his time to anyone who wished to talk with him, remarking that he was surprised by the fact that if he had claimed to be a physician for the teeth, everybody would flock to him who needed to have a tooth pulled. Yes, and by Zeus, if he had professed to treat the eyes, all who were suffering from sore eyes would present themselves. And similarly, if he had claimed to know of a medicine for diseases of the spleen or for gout or for a runny nose.

But when he declared that all who followed his treatment would be relieved of ignorance, wickedness, and licentiousness, not one person would listen to him or seek to be cured by him—no matter how much richer he might become thereby. It was as though they were less inconvenienced by these spiritual complaints than by the other kind. Or as though it were worse for them to suffer from an enlarged spleen or a decayed tooth than from a soul that is foolish, ignorant, cowardly, rash, pleasure-loving, unfree, prone to anger, unkind, and wicked—in fact, utterly corrupt.—DC

5. Diogenes was amazed that literary scholars investigate Odysseus' misfortunes while they are ignorant of their own. And that musicians tune their lyre's strings while their soul's disposition and habits are out of tune. And that mathematicians gaze at the sun and the moon but overlook matters close at hand. And that orators are so zealous and serious when they speak about justice, but they never practice it. And that those who are greedy blame everything on money while loving it excessively.—DL

6. We must look into the good and bad done in our own households.—DDL

7. Observing a foolish man tuning a harp, Diogenes said, "Are you not ashamed to give this piece of wood harmonious sounds while you fail to harmonize your soul with your life?" —DDL

8. It is enough to listen to the Pythian god when he counsels, "Know yourself." —J

Endurance

1. The Cynic should have such power of endurance that he seems insensible to the common sort, like a stone. —EP

2. Antisthenes used to walk about five miles to Athens every day in order to hear Socrates. He learned the art of endurance from him, imitating his indifference to suffering. So it was that he began the Cynic philosophy and the Cynic way of life. —DL

3. Antisthenes led the way in terms of Diogenes' indifference to suffering, Crates' self-control, and Zeno's patient endurance. —DL

4. We are called Cynics not because we are indifferent to things but because we doggedly stick with things that are unbearable to others on account of softness and mere opinions. . . . Stand your ground, therefore, and practice Cynicism with me. . . . Pursue not only the best of goods, self-control and endurance, but also what produces them, hard work and toil. —LC

5. For this very amusing quality is tied to a Cynic: he

must be flogged like a donkey, and when he is flogged, he must love those who flog him as if he were the father and the brother of all. . . . No man reviles the Cynic, no man strikes him, no man insults him—but he gives his body up so that any man who chooses may do with it what he likes.—EP

6. As for me, . . . I can put up with cold and heat, and I am not displeased with the works of the gods.—LS

7. In summertime, Diogenes used to roll in his wine-jar house over hot sand. And in wintertime, he used to hug statues of men covered with snow. He practiced endurance in every way.—DL

8. To those who said to him, "You are an old man, you should take a break and rest," Diogenes replied, "Why? If I were running a long race, should I slow down when I was near the finish line? Should I not endure to the end?"—DDL

9. To Epimenides, greetings: You stay at home delighting your belly and adorning your body instead of enduring by means of virtue.—LD

10. When Diogenes was sold as a slave, he endured it most nobly.—DL

Hard Work

1. Hard work, with all its toil and suffering, is something good. —ADL

2. Be persuaded that working hard is the reason why one does not have to work hard. —LC

3. Whether you want to work hard or you want to avoid working hard, work hard. This way you won't be working hard. Why? Because when you slack off you're not actually avoiding hard work; rather, you're making things harder. —LC

4. Pursue not only the best of goods, self-control and endurance, but also what produces them, hard work and toil. —LC

5. Get used to washing in cold water, drinking water, and eating nothing that has not come to you by means of toil and sweat. —LC

6. You find fault with my life for how hard and toilsome it is, and that no one will practice it because it is so difficult and harsh. But I have increased its

difficulty on purpose so that those who imitate me might know not to enjoy fine things. —DL

18

SUFFERING & HARDSHIP

1. Diogenes freely submitted his body to toil and hardships so that he might make it stronger than it was by nature. —J

2. I, superior to the hardships, chose the steep and troublesome path. —LD

3. Diogenes was not in the habit of giving himself over to drowsiness and sleep. —DL

4. Diogenes would walk in the snow barefoot. —DL

5. Crates would wear a cloak thick with hair during the summer and a tattered one during the winter. —DL

6. Listen to what Diogenes says to the passersby when he had a fever. "Miserable wretches—will you not stay? But are you going on so long a journey to Olympia to see the destruction or the fight of athletes? And will you not choose to see the battle between a fever and a man?" —EP

7. When a certain man asked whether Diogenes had

also come to see the contest at the Isthmian games, he responded, "No, but to take part." Then when the man laughed and asked him who his competitors were, he said with that customary glance of his, "The toughest there are and the hardest to beat—men whom no Greek can look straight in the eye. They are not competitors, however, who sprint or wrestle or jump, or those who box and throw the spear and hurl the discus, but those that correct and chasten a man." The other asked, "Tell me, who are they?" He replied, "Hardships that are very severe and impossible to overcome for gluttonous and folly-stricken men who feast all day long and snore at night, but which yield to thin, spare men, whose waists are more pinched in than those of wasps." —DC

8. Diogenes said, "The noble and excellent man believes that his hardships are his greatest opponents, and always wants to battle with them day and night—not to win a sprig of parsley, as so many goats might do, nor for a bit of wild olive, or of pine, but to win happiness and virtue throughout all the days of his life. . . . He is afraid of none of those opponents nor does he pray to draw another, but he challenges them one after another, grappling with hunger and cold, withstanding thirst, and disclosing no weakness even though he must endure the lash or give his body to be

cut or burned. Poverty, exile, loss of reputation, and the like have no terrors for him. No, he holds them as mere trifles, and while in their grip, the perfect man is often as sportive as boys with their dice and their colored balls." —DC

9. "Of course," Diogenes continued, "these antagonists do seem terrible and invincible to all who are bad men. But if you treat them with contempt and meet them boldly, you will find them cowardly and unable to master strong men. In this way these opponents very much resemble dogs that pursue and bite people who run away from them, while some they seize and tear to pieces. On the other hand, they fear and slink away from men who face them and show them a fight, eventually wagging their tails when they come to know them. Most people, however, are in mortal terror of these opponents, always avoiding them by flight and never looking them in the face. It is no different from skillful boxers. They are not hit at all when they anticipate their opponents; rather, they often actually end up winning the match themselves. On the contrary, if they give ground through fear, they receive the heaviest blow. In the same way, if we accept our hardships in a spirit of contempt for them and approach them cheerfully, they avail very little against us. But if we hang back and give way, they

appear altogether greater and stronger." —DC

10. If anyone wishes to weigh every stage in the whole of life, he will discover that there is a far greater quantity of pain and suffering. —T

11. Pleasure, after overpowering and taking possession of her victims, delivers them over to the most hateful and most difficult hardships. —DC

12. Pleasure also brings diverse and deadly vipers into being, and other crawling things that are always with her as they stand by her doors. And though yearning for pleasure and serving her, they nevertheless suffer countless hardships and suffering all in vain. —DC

DESIRE & DESIRE REDUCTION

1. Diogenes used to say that it was characteristic of the gods to need nothing, and that, consequently, when a man desires very little or nothing at all, he is like the gods. —DL

2. My life is that of a decent, well-behaved man. . . . I enjoy what comes to hand, use what is cheap, and have no desire for the elaborate and exotic. —LS

3. In response to the man who asked, "What will it mean for me to do philosophy?" Crates said, "You will live satisfied with what you have, neither desiring what is absent nor being displeased with whatever comes your way." —T

4. May I have no need—I nor any that I call friend—for gold and silver. For every human misfortune is generated by a longing for these—civil strife and wars, conspiracies and slaughters. The fountain of them all is a longing for more. That's not me. May I bear with less rather than desiring more and more. —LS

5. If a thing doesn't free a man from insatiate desire

and stinginess and false pretension, then neither does it free him from need and scarcity. But no amount of wealth frees a man from insatiate desire and stinginess and false pretension since it does not change his character or his habits. —T

6. It seems to me someone could sooner say that the acquisition of wealth changes skin color, body size, or appearance than it does character. But so long as this man is insatiable, stingy, pretentious, and wretched, he will experience need and scarcity. —T

7. By the easiest means, the Cynic must satisfy his body's needs so long as the god commands him to use it as an instrument. —J

8. If you think I live the life of an animal just because I need and use only a few things, that argument leads you to the conclusion that the gods are even lower than animals are since the gods have no needs at all. . . . The gods have no needs, and those men who have the fewest needs are nearest the gods. —LS

9. The Cynic avoids excessive or extravagant food. He turns away from sex, from those things that belong to Aphrodite. When overpowered by the needs of the body, he does not cling to reputation, nor does he wait

around for a cook and sauces and a savory smell, nor does he ever look around for *prostitutes like* Phryne or Lais or for So-and-so's wife or young daughter or serving-maid. But as far as possible, he satisfies his body's needs with whatever he happens to find. And by thrusting aside the body's troubles, he looks down from above, from the peaks of Olympus, at other men who are "wandering in darkness in the meadows of Bewilderment"—those who are, for the sake of a few wholly trifling enjoyments, undergoing torments greater than any by the Cocytus or Acheron, those such as the most ingenious of the poets are always telling us about.—J

10. Do you see that people persuade the young to love wealth, to hate poverty, to take care of the belly, to endure any toil for the body's sake, to fatten that prison of the soul, to keep up an expensive table, never to sleep alone at night, provided only that they do all this in the dark and are not discovered? Is not this worse than Tartarus?—J

11. There is a story of a man on a vicious horse that describes your situation. The horse ran away with him, and at the pace it was going, he could not get off. A man in the way asked him where he was off to. "Wherever this animal takes me," he said. So if one asked you where you were going, if you cared to tell the truth,

you would say, generally speaking, wherever your longings decide to go. Or, more specifically, you would say, wherever your pleasure decides to go. Or at times greed. Or anger. Or fear. Or at other times some other thing appears to carry you off. You're not just on one horse. No, you're mounted on many that carry you. And they're all mad with passion! They carry you toward pits and cliffs, but you do not realize that you are bound for a fall until the fall itself comes. —LS

12. Rid yourself of every passion by means of holy philosophy. —LD

13. Bad men obey their desires as house slaves obey their masters. —DDL

14. Poverty does not consist in not having money, nor is begging something bad. Instead, poverty consists in desiring everything. —LD

15. You behave randomly in your own affairs, never acting as a result of deliberation or reason, but always thanks to habit and longing. You are no better than people washed around by a flood. They drift with the current, and you with your longings. —LS

16. Is it not better to sink beneath Charybdis and

Cocytus or countless fathoms beneath the earth than to fall into a life like this, enslaved to your genitals and your belly?—J

17. Never think, my friend, that you are free while your belly rules you, and the part below the belly, since you will then have masters who can either furnish you the means of pleasure or deprive you of them.—J

18. Diogenes called the belly the Charybdis of one's livelihood.—DL

19. Let him who wishes to be a Cynic, to be an excellent man, first take himself in hand like Diogenes and Crates, and expel the passions from his own soul and from every part of it. And let him entrust all his affairs to reason and intelligence and steer his course by them—for this was the central point, I suppose, of Diogenes' philosophy.—J

20. The self-sufficient and simple soul has been purified of vice and has been released from empty opinion. It has cast out immoderate desires and has been taught to speak the truth and to show contempt for other false things. If you are not persuaded by this, then practice the love of pleasure.—LD

21. In the things that relate to you, you must not in any way be what you are like now. You must not blame God or man. You must take away desire altogether. And you must avoid only the things that are within the power of the will. You must not feel anger or resentment or envy or pity. A girl must not appear pretty to you. And you mustn't love a little reputation. And you mustn't be pleased with a boy or a cake. —EP

22. The poets tell that Hercules of old by his valor subdued all the wild monsters of legend, beast or man, and purged all the world of them. Even so our philosopher Crates was truly a Hercules in the conquest of anger, envy, avarice, lust, and all the other monstrous and shameful things that plague the human soul. He expelled all these pests from their minds, purged households, and tamed vice. —AP

23. To Perdiccas: If you are presently fighting against opinions and appearances, enemies which, I say, are stronger and harm you more than both the Thracians and Paeonians, and if you are working to subdue the human passions, then send for me. I say this because I am able to battle against these as a general does. —LD

Self-Control

1. When Phryne the prostitute set up a golden statue of Aphrodite in Delphi, Diogenes is said to have written on it, "From Greece's lack of self-control." —DL

2. Desire is a disease of the soul, whereas health is self-control. —B

3. Pursue not only the best of goods, self-control and endurance, but also what produces them, hard work and toil. —LC

4. They say that men become three times happy as three goods multiply in their lives. How could those who have a self-controlled soul, a healthy body, and independence relative to possessions not be three times happy? —LC

5. Antisthenes led the way in terms of Diogenes' indifference to suffering, Crates' self-control, and Zeno's patient endurance. —DL

6. Take Heracles, the best man that ever lived, a divine man, and rightly considered a god. Was it unhappiness

that made him go around in nothing but a lion's skin, insensible to all the needs you feel? . . . Do you suppose, then, that he could not get coverings or clothes or shoes, and that's why he went around as he did? We cannot draw this conclusion. Rather, he possessed self-control and was able to endure. He wanted to be powerful, strong. He didn't want luxury. —LS

7. God seems to be self-control because he desires nothing. —B

21

SEX & SEXUAL DESIRE

1. Sexual love is the business of those with nothing to do. —DDL

2. Never think, my friend, that you are free while your belly rules you, and the part below the belly, since you will then have masters who can either furnish you the means of pleasure or deprive you of them. . . . Is it not better to sink beneath Charybdis and Cocytus or countless fathoms beneath the earth than to fall into a life like this, enslaved to your genitals and your belly? . . . The Cynic turns away from sex, from those things that belong to Aphrodite. When overpowered by the needs of the body, he never looks around for *prostitutes like* Phryne or Lais or for So-and-so's wife or young daughter or serving-maid. —J

3. Such is this thing pleasure, which hatches no single plot but all kinds of plots, and aims to undo men through sight, sound, smell, taste, and touch, with food too, and drink and sexual lust, tempting alike those awake and those asleep. —DC

4. Hunger puts a stop to sexual desire. And if not

hunger, then time. And if both these fail, then a noose. —CDL

5. Diogenes said that the pleasure shared by lovers is their own misfortune. —DL

6. Diogenes compared prostitutes to deadly honeyed potions. . . . To the man who was earnestly entreating a prostitute, Diogenes said, "Why, miserable man, do you want success when it would be better for you to be unsuccessful?" . . . When Diogenes saw a man who had been a victor at the Olympian games looking again and again at a prostitute, he said, "Look at that warlike ram who is overpowered by the first girl he happens to meet." —DDL

7. Adulterous relationships belong to the realm of tragedy. They end with exile and murder. —CDL

8. One day, when Antisthenes saw an adulterer running for his life, he said, "Wretched man! What a great amount of danger you might have avoided at the price of an obol." —DL

9. The one who is free from the passions and supposes his own property is enough for patient endurance shuns marriage and producing offspring. —LD

22

PLEASURE

1. If the happy life must be measured by the yardstick of excessive pleasure, then no one, says Crates, will be judged happy. —T

2. I do not see how someone will live a happy life if he really must measure it by an excess of pleasure. —T

3. If you become someone who looks down on pleasure, and someone who doesn't set himself against hard work, and someone who considers equal both good and bad reputation, and someone who doesn't fear death, then it will be possible for you to do whatever you wish without suffering distress. —T

4. According to Diogenes, contempt for pleasure is, if we get used to it, quite pleasant itself. And just as those who are accustomed to living with pleasure feel nauseous when they have to give this life up, so too do those who have practiced the opposite life feel pleasure when they look down on pleasure. —DL

5. Flee not only from the worst of the vices, injustice and a lack of self-control, but also what produces

them, pleasure and enjoyment. —LC

6. There is a battle even more terrible, a struggle that is no small thing … I mean the fight against pleasure. —DC

7. Pleasure uses no open force but deceives and casts a spell with baneful drugs, just as Homer says Circe drugged the comrades of Odysseus, and some straightaway became swine, some wolves, and some other kinds of beasts. —DC

8. When pleasure gains dominion and overpowers the soul by means of her charms, her enchanted drugs, the rest of Circe's sorcery at once follows. With a stroke of her wand pleasure coolly drives her victim into a sort of pigsty and pens him up. And now, from that time on, the man goes on living as a pig or a wolf. —DC

9. Pleasure carries us off to shameful deeds. —LD

10. To a handsome young man who was going to a drinking party, Diogenes said, "You will return a worse man." —DL

11. Pleasure, after overpowering and taking possession of her victims, delivers them over to the most hateful and most difficult hardships. —DC

12. Pleasure also brings diverse and deadly vipers into being, and other crawling things that are always with her as they stand by her doors. And though yearning for pleasure and serving her, they nevertheless suffer countless hardships and suffering all in vain.—DC

13. Pain and hardship come by means of touch for the most part and continue in that way, but pleasure assails a man through each and every sense that he has.—DC

14. Such is this thing pleasure, which hatches no single plot but all kinds of plots, and aims to undo men through sight, sound, smell, taste, and touch, with food too, and drink and sexual lust, tempting alike those awake and those asleep.—DC

15. It is not possible to station guards and then lie down to sleep as in ordinary warfare. No, it is just then of all times that pleasure makes her attack—at one time weakening and enslaving the soul by means of sleep itself, at another sending mischievous and insidious dreams that bring her to mind.—DC

16. While a man must face and grapple with pain and hardship, he should flee from pleasure as far as possible and only have unavoidable dealings with her.—DC

17. Here the strongest man is more or less the most excellent man, the one who is able to flee the greatest distance away from pleasure—for it is impossible to dwell with pleasure or even to linger with her for any length of time without being wholly conquered and enslaved.—DC

18. Diogenes said that the pleasure shared by lovers is their own misfortune.—DL

23

Self-Sufficiency & Contentment

1. Diogenes used to teach the boys in his care to supply their own needs, and to be content with simple food and water to drink. He further accustomed them to cutting their hair close to the skin, and to shun fashionable adornments, and to go out with fewer clothes on and no shoes, and to walk along the way silently and without looking around. —DL

2. Do not be distressed, father, that I call myself a dog, and I clothe myself with a doubled over, tattered cloak, and I carry a leather bag over my shoulders, and I have a staff in my hand. It's not fitting to be upset by such matters. Instead, be delighted that your son is content with little. —LD

3. A man's sufficiency is that which meets his needs. . . . Want or lacking occurs when the supply falls short of need and does not satisfy what is needful. . . . So then, I am lacking nothing—I am not in want. Everything I have is lined up with what I require. —LS

4. To Apolexis, greetings: I spoke with you about a place to live. Thank you for taking this on. But when

I beheld a snail, I found a house that would keep off the wind—that is, the wine jar in the Mētrōon. So then I release you from this service. Let us rejoice over this discovery of nature.—LD

5. Diogenes revealed to mortal men the teaching that self-sufficient living is a way of life that is not burdensome.—DL

6. When Metrocles switched over to Crates, . . . he became simple in his character and habits, satisfied with a tattered cloak and barley bread and vegetables, neither yearning after his earlier way of life nor vexed by the present.—T

7. As for me, my possessions are so great that I can hardly find them myself. I have enough to eat so that I'm not hungry and enough to drink so that I'm not thirsty. And I have enough clothing so that when I'm outside, I'm no colder than Callias is, a man who is remarkably wealthy. And when I go into a house, I look on the walls as exceedingly warm tunics and the roofs as exceptionally thick mantles. And the bedding that I own is so satisfactory that it is actually a hard task to wake me up in the morning.—AX

8. The most valuable part of my wealth I count as this,

that even if someone robbed me of what I now possess, I see no occupation so humble that it would not furnish me with adequate provisions. For whenever I wish to enjoy myself, I do not purchase highly prized items in the marketplace since they are very expensive, but I withdraw wealth from my soul. —AX

9. It is natural that those whose eyes are set on frugality are more honest than those whose eyes are fixed on money-making. For those who are most contented with what they have are least likely to covet what belongs to others. —AX

10. In response to the man who asked, "What will it mean for me to do philosophy?" Crates said, "You will live satisfied with what you have, neither desiring what is absent nor being displeased with whatever comes your way." —T

11. As for me, my feet take me anywhere I want to go. I can put up with cold and heat, and I am not displeased with the works of the gods —LS

12. What enemy would march against one who is self-sufficient and simple? And against which king or people would those satisfied with these things carry on a war? In conformity with this, the soul has been

purified of vice and has been released from empty opinion. It has cast out immoderate desires and has been taught to speak the truth and to show contempt for other false things. If you are not persuaded by this, then practice the love of pleasure. —LD

13. We are not able to be content with our present circumstances when we devote ourselves excessively to luxury and when we judge work a misfortune and death the worst of evils. —T

14. But far as possible, the Cynic satisfies his body's needs with whatever he happens to find. —J

15. I praise those who were about to marry—and didn't. And those who were going to go on a voyage—and didn't. And those who were about to engage in politics—and didn't. And those who were going to have and raise a family—and didn't. And those who were about to move in with rulers—and didn't. —DDL

16. When he was asked what wine he found pleasant to drink, he replied, "Wine that another man provides." —DDL

24

CIRCUMSTANCES

1. Diogenes was a man who gloried in his circumstances. —EP

2. It was by watching a mouse—how it didn't long for a marriage bed, and how it didn't care about the dark, and how it didn't long for things that have a reputation for causing pleasure—that Diogenes discovered the means of adapting himself to circumstances. —DL

3. We are not able to be content with our present circumstances when we devote ourselves excessively to luxury and when we judge work a misfortune and death the worst of evils. —T

4. Many mad men lay the blame on circumstances rather than on themselves. . . . We blame everything else more than we do our own irritability and unhappiness. We blame old age, poverty, chance encounters, the day, the season, the place. —T

5. You are displeased with everything that happens and grumble without ceasing. What is, is intolerable. What is not, you pine for. In winter you want

summer; in summer, winter. In heat you pine for cold; in cold, for heat. You're as fastidious and peevish as invalids are—only their reason is to be found in their illness, whereas yours is in your way of life.—LS

6. I do not see how circumstances themselves involve anything troublesome—neither old age nor poverty nor if one is foreign.—T

7. It is not the city that is cheap or very expensive; rather, if one lives one way it is very expensive, and if one lives another way it is cheap. So it is with circumstances. If someone makes use of them in one way, they appear favorable and easy. But if in another way, unmanageable, annoying.—T

8. I've concluded from my own life that we human beings are distressed whenever we wish to live a problem-free life. But this is impossible! For by necessity we live with the body, and by necessity we also live with human beings.—LC

9. To the point and suitable in every circumstance, my honored man, is the oracle of the ancients that says, "Do not flee from those things that are necessary." I say this because the one who flees from what is necessary is inevitably unhappy.—LC

24 • CIRCUMSTANCES

10. One should not attempt to change circumstances; rather, one should get ready for them as they are. Do this as sailors do. They don't try to change the winds and the sea. Instead, they ready themselves so that they are able to respond to these things. —T

11. Just as I am able to transfer from one ship to another and have a comparably good voyage, so I am able to move from one city to another and be equally happy. —T

12. Bion puts it this way: just as when you catch a wild animal, you may be bitten, so too if you take hold of a snake by the middle, you'll be bitten, but if you do so by the throat, then nothing will happen. It's the same with circumstances, he says. If you take them one way, you may experience distress. Yet if you take them in the same way as Socrates, you will not suffer. But if in any other way, then you will feel distress, not because of circumstances but because of your own character and your own false views. —T

13. For me life is so unreliable and uncertain that I cannot rely on lasting here until I finish writing this letter to you. —LD

14. The body is nothing to me. Its parts are nothing to

me. And death? Let it come when it chooses—either death of the whole or some part. And exile? To where? Does any man have the power to throw me out of the cosmos? No, he can't. Wherever I go, there is the sun, there is the moon, there are the stars, dreams, omens, and communion with the gods.—EP

15. How, then, is it possible that anything that belongs to the body can be free from hindrance? And how is a thing great or valuable that is naturally dead, earth, or mud?—EP

16. As when the enemy press upon you, hurling their weapons, you retreat to camp since you are fighting bare of armor, so when a war-like fight presses upon you at times—a lack of resources, a poor state of health—retreat to one meal per day, to self-service, to a tattered cloak, and, finally, to Hades.—T

17. To be free from passion is the very thing that a blessed man should be so that he does not feel grief over the death of a friend or child or even over the end his own life.—T

25

FORTUNE, CHANCE, LUCK (*TYCHĒ*)*

1. Entrust nothing to Fortune (Chance, Luck). —DL

2. When someone asked him what result he obtained from philosophy, he said, "If nothing else, this: I am prepared for every turn of Fortune." —DDL

3. I am able to counter Fortune with courage. —DDL

4. The Cynics were so far from bearing with a bad grace any threat of Fortune, whether one call such threats caprice or wanton insult, that once when he had been captured by pirates Diogenes joked with them. As for Crates, he gave his property to the state, and being physically deformed, he made light of his own disabled leg and curved shoulders. —J

5. Just as a good actor must contend well for the victory with the mask and role that the playwright gives him, so also must a good man compete with the one that Fortune gives him. For Bion says that Fortune, like a playwright, sometimes gives the mask and role of a first-speaker (leading role) and sometimes that of a second-speaker (supporting role). And sometimes a

king, and sometimes a wandering beggar. So, when you are a second-speaker, do not wish for the mask and role of a first-speaker. Otherwise, you will do something unsuitable. —T

6. Fortune, as though a playwright, makes up roles of every kind: a shipwrecked man, a beggar, an exile, a well-regarded man, and one disreputable. A good man should, therefore, contend well with whatever role that Fortune gives him. You have become shipwrecked—play the shipwreck well. From being well-off you have become poor—play the poor man well. . . . Be satisfied with any clothing, food, and service that happen to come along, as was Laertes . . . For these things are enough for living suitably and healthily, unless someone wishes to live luxuriously. —T

---

* In the ancient world, *tychē* (fortune, chance, luck) was a power or force that led in one direction or another, whether toward benefit or harm. Sometimes the power was judged divine—a goddess. Thus, the capital letter. She was *Tychē*, the personification of Fortune, Chance, or Luck—the power behind private or public success. In Rome, she was known as the goddess *Fortuna*. Where you see "Fortune" in each point, read *Tychē* or *tychē*.

Wealth

1. The love of money is the mother-city, the origin, of all evils.—DDL

2. May I have no need—I nor any that I call friend—for gold and silver. For every human misfortune is generated by a longing for these—civil strife and wars, conspiracies and slaughters. The fountain of them all is a longing for more. That's not me. May I bear with less rather than desiring more and more.—LS

3. Wealth is harmful if it is not used in a worthwhile manner.—MDL

4. Most of the precious instruments of happiness that you so pride yourselves on are won only with unhappiness and hardships. Give a moment's thought, if you will, to the gold you all pray for, to the silver, the costly houses, the elaborate clothing. And do not forget all the trouble and toil and danger they cost—the blood and death and ruin. Not only do large numbers of men perish at sea on their account, but many endure miseries in producing them. Moreover, they're very likely to be fought for—the desire for them

makes friends plot against friends, children against parents, wives against husbands. —LS

5. Socrates said, "And you, Antisthenes, what do you pride yourself on?"

"I pride myself on wealth," he declared. . . .

"Okay, then," Socrates went on, "given the little wealth that you have, tell us how you pride yourself on wealth."

"I do because I believe that a man's wealth or lack of wealth is not a matter of household goods but of soul goods. I observe many private citizens who think of themselves as poor even though they have a pile of money and possessions. For this reason they give themselves over to any toil or danger in order to increase their wealth. And I know of brothers who have an equal share of their inheritance. One of them has plenty, more than enough to meet expenses, while the other is in utter want. And I've observed some tyrants who are so hungry for wealth that they are willing to do terrible things compared with those who are entirely poor. Because they lack things, some people snatch things, others break in and take things, and others follow the slave trade. But there are some tyrants who destroy whole families, kill men by the crowd, and oftentimes enslave even entire cities, all for the sake of money. I deeply pity these men for this oppressive disease. They are like the man who has plenty to eat but can't satisfy himself even though he keeps on eating." —AX

6. Wealth of this kind also makes people generous. My friend Socrates here and I are examples. For Socrates, from whom I acquired this wealth of mine, did not come to my relief limiting it by number and weight, but he gave me all that I could carry. And as for me, I am now stingy with no one; rather, I openly display my abundance to all my friends and share my soul wealth with anyone who desires it. —AX

7. Much wealth is prey to vanity. —CDL

8. When Crates understood that the wealth that had been given to him came with no safeguard on which he might lean as on a staff in the course of his life, he realized that all was fragile and transitory—that all the wealth in all the world was no help in living well, in living virtuously. —AP

9. I've learned that you carried all your property to the assembly and handed it over to your fatherland. Standing amid the assembly, you proclaimed, "Crates, the son of Crates, sets Crates free." —LD

10. One might say that it seems the acquisition of wealth releases one from scarcity and need. And how is that? Don't you see that some people have acquired much—as appearances go, anyway—and yet they don't use it because of stinginess and meanness.

11. If a thing doesn't free a man from insatiate desire and stinginess and false pretension, then neither does it free him from need and scarcity. But no amount of wealth frees a man from insatiate desire and stinginess and false pretension since it does not change his character or his habits. —T

12. If Euremus truly grew up with virtue, then he should have never introduced into himself a desire for money, which is the cause of every evil. —LD

13. It seems to me someone could sooner say that the acquisition of wealth changes skin color, body size, or appearance than it does character. But so long as this man is insatiable, stingy, pretentious, and wretched, he will experience need and scarcity. —T

14. Metrocles divided things in the following manner: those things that are obtained with money, such as a house, and those things that are obtained with time and care, such as an education. —DL

15. Diogenes said that very valuable things were sold for worthless things—and the other way around. Accordingly, a statue goes for three thousand, while a measure of barley meal is sold for two copper coins. —DL

Poverty

1. Poverty does not consist in not having money, nor is begging something bad. Instead, poverty consists in desiring everything. —LD

2. Crates of Thebes declared that obscurity and poverty were his own homeland, which Fortune could never take captive. —DL

3. Many mad men lay the blame on circumstances rather than on themselves.... We blame everything else more than we do our own irritability and unhappiness. We blame old age, poverty, chance encounters, the day, the season, the place. —T

4. *How is poverty annoying or painful?* Did not Crates and Diogenes easily carry on when they gave up arrogance and became beggars and developed the ability to make use of a cheap and simple way of life. —T

5. There are few natures, whether of body or soul, that are able to pass over from an inferior life to one of unmixed good—though such a nature did belong to the Cynics Diogenes of Sinope and Crates of Thebes ... and

people like that.... It was when these Cynics were reduced to poverty that they genuinely pursued philosophy. It was then they began to live a truly human life according to nature, demonstrating the true wealth found in the simple life.—SIMPLICIUS

6. The following line tells us what Crates of Thebes gained from philosophy: "A measure of lupin beans and no one to worry about."—DL

7. In response to the man who asked, "What will it mean for me to do philosophy?" Crates said, "You will easily be able to open your bag and freely give from it rather than, as now, writhing and irresolute and shaking as men do with disabled hands.... If you notice that your bag is empty, you will not suffer distress.... You will live satisfied with what you have, neither desiring what is absent nor being displeased with whatever comes your way.—T

8. When Metrocles of Maroneia switched over to Crates, there was none of these things (*the right shoes, clothes, servants, house, food, wine, and entertainment*). Rather, he became simple in his character and habits, satisfied with a tattered cloak and barley bread and vegetables, neither yearning after his earlier way of life nor vexed by the present.—T

9. The ancients put it well: if a thing doesn't free a man from insatiate desire and stinginess and false pretension, then neither does it free him from need and scarcity. But no amount of wealth frees a man from insatiate desire and stinginess and false pretension since it does not change his character or his habits. For instance, not even poverty will change the character of those who are moderate if they become poor after being rich. It seems to me someone could sooner say that the acquisition of wealth changes skin color, body size, or appearance than it does character. But so long as this man is insatiable, stingy, pretentious, and wretched, he will experience need and scarcity. —T

10. *Diogenes of Sinope said,* "The noble and excellent man believes that his hardships are his greatest opponents, and always wants to battle with them day and night — not to win a sprig of parsley, as so many goats might do, nor for a bit of wild olive, or of pine, but to win happiness and virtue throughout all the days of his life. . . . He is afraid of none of those opponents nor does he pray to draw another, but he challenges them one after another, grappling with hunger and cold, withstanding thirst, and disclosing no weakness even though he must endure the lash or give his body to be cut or burned. Poverty, exile, loss of reputation, and the like have no terrors for him." —DC

11. Poverty would say to the man who brought a charge against her, "Why do you battle me? Do I rob you of anything good? I don't, do I? Not of moderation. Not of justice. Not of courage—do I? Are you lacking anything necessary for life? Are not the roads full of vegetables and the springs full of water? Do I not furnish you with as many beds as the earth does? As well as leaves for bedding? Or is it not possible to delight in me? Or don't you see old women eating cheap barley cakes and talking away? Or don't I provide you with hunger—a season that costs nothing and is not effeminate? Or is it not the case that a hungry person most enjoys eating and least misses the seasoning?—and that a thirsty person most enjoys drinking and least awaits the drink that is not by his side?" —T

12. It is not accurate to say that poverty hinders one from doing philosophy whereas wealth is useful. For how many men do you suppose have been kept from the leisure necessary for philosophy thanks to an abundance of wealth as compared to those lacking wealth?—T

13. When you train to look down on poverty, a bad reputation, low birth, and exile, you will live blessedly. . . . Otherwise, you will live miserably. —LD

14. *Diogenes relates the counsel he gave to a man in Cyzicus*

who, like everyone else, had the following inscription written upon his door: The child of Zeus, the gloriously triumphant Heracles, lives here, may no bad thing enter— things such as sickness, poverty, death.

If the inscription is so helpful, asked Diogenes, then why don't you have it written upon your city gates? Or what about the marketplace? Or why not upon yourselves?

When the man asked him what other inscription would be better, Diogenes suggested that it would be far better to inscribe: "Poverty lives here, may no bad thing enter."

"Say something good, man!" he said. "But this itself is something bad." . . .

"What does it do that you say it is a bad thing?" Diogenes said.

"Poverty is responsible for hunger," he said, "and cold and contempt."

Diogenes denied that poverty is responsible for these. "Poverty is not responsible for harmful things; rather, wickedness is. And what else," he said, "would poverty accomplish if it lived with you? Would poverty not be chosen when it drove other even stronger, more violent bad things away from you?"

"What kind of bad things?" he asked.

"Jealousies, hatreds, false accusations, people breaking into other people's houses, indigestion, colic—other painful afflictions. Write, therefore, that poverty lives among you and not Heracles. For you are not afraid of the things that Heracles is able to destroy: water serpents, bulls, lions, kerberos dogs. . . . But whatever poverty drives away, these are fearful." —LD

15. People persuade the young to love wealth, to hate poverty, to take care of the belly, to endure any toil for the body's sake, to fatten that prison of the soul. —J

THINGS INDIFFERENT

1. The Cynics teach that whatever is between virtue and vice should be counted as indifferent, that is, neither good nor bad. —DL

> *Why do the Cynics hold that "whatever is between virtue and vice should be counted as indifferent"? For the following reasons—*

2. Virtue is sufficient for happiness. —ADL

3. We Cynics say that the good and excellent man, and no other man, is called happy. —LC

4. Virtue alone is that by which the soul can be strengthened and delivered from its afflictions. —LD

SIMPLICITY, FRUGALITY & LIVING SIMPLY

1. Diogenes of Sinope set out to live a simple and frugal life. . . . Some say that he was the first to fold over his cloak. This was necessary because he slept in it. He carried a leather bag that held his food. He used any place for any purpose—eating, sleeping, and talking with others.—DL

2. Cynics teach that men should live simply, procuring for themselves only necessary food and wearing only one piece of clothing, a worn garment. They think very little of wealth and reputation and noble birth. Some Cynics get by on herbs and vegetables and cold water. They live in any kind of shelter, or even large wine-jars, just as did Diogenes, who used to say that it was characteristic of the gods to need nothing, and that, consequently, when a man desires very little or nothing at all, he is like the gods.—DL

3. You who possess everything have nothing thanks to your love of strife and jealousy and fear and vanity. You commit treachery and behave as a tyrant and murder. By contrast we Cynics are completely at peace—free from every bad thing thanks to Diogenes of Sinope.

Although we have nothing, we have everything. —LC

4. When someone extolled a luxurious life, Antisthenes said, "May the sons of your enemies have a luxurious life!" —ADL

5. How pointless it all is! Embroidered clothes have no more warmth in them than others. Gilded houses do not do better in keeping out the rain. A drink is no sweeter out of a silver cup—or a gold one for that matter. An ivory bed makes sleep no softer; on the contrary, your fortunate man on his ivory bed between his delicate sheets constantly finds himself calling on sleep in vain. And as to the elaborate preparation of food, I hardly need to say that instead of aiding nutrition it injures the body and produces diseases in it. —LS

6. Bread, water, a bed of straw, and a tattered cloak teach moderation and patient endurance. —LD

7. It is not among men who eat bread that you will find tyrants but among those who feast lavishly. —DDL

8. When the Macedonian general Craterus demanded that he come and visit him, Diogenes said, "I would rather live on a few grains of salt in Athens than enjoy a table full of costly food with Craterus." —DDL

9. The gods gave men an easy life. But the easy life became obscure over time by their seeking honey-cakes and perfumes and like things. —DDL

10. To Apolexis, greetings: I spoke with you about a place to live. Thank you for taking this on. But when I beheld a snail, I found a house that would keep off the wind—that is, the wine jar in the Mētrōon. —LD

11. Take care of your soul—but your body only so far as what is necessary, and externals not even that much. I say this because happiness is not a pleasure that requires external things. —LC

12. A man's wealth or lack of wealth is not a matter of household goods but of soul goods. —AX

13. Crates and Diogenes easily carried on when they gave up arrogance and became beggars and developed the ability to make use of a cheap and simple way of life. —T

14. Crates wrote a hymn to Thrift: "Greetings, goddess queen, the delight of wise men, Thrift, the child of glorious Moderation." —J

15. When Metrocles switched over to Crates, . . . he

became simple in his character and habits, satisfied with a tattered cloak and barley bread and vegetables, neither yearning after his earlier way of life nor vexed by the present. —T

16. Poverty would say to the man who brought a charge against her, "Why do you battle me? Do I rob you of anything good? I don't, do I? Not of moderation. Not of justice. Not of courage, do I?" —T

17. The right travelling supplies for a journey are such that, even if you are shipwrecked, you will be able to swim with them. —ADL

18. Demetrius of Magnesia tells a story that Crates deposited his money with a banker, making the following agreement with him. If his sons became ordinary people, then he was to give the money to them. But if they became philosophers, then he was to apportion it among the people, since his sons would need nothing if they were philosophers. —DL

19. And how is it possible that a man who has nothing—who is naked, houseless, and without a hearth, who is squalid, without a slave or a city—how can such a man pass a life that flows well? Behold, God has sent you a man to show you that it is possible:

"Look at me," the Cynic says, "I who am without a city, without a house, without possessions, without a slave. I sleep on the ground. I have no wife, no children, no praetorium; rather, I have only the earth and the heavens, and one poor cloak. And what do I want? Am I not without pain and sorrow? Without fear? Am I not free? When did any of you see me failing in the object of my desire? Or ever falling into what I would rather avoid? Did I ever blame God or man? Did I ever accuse anyone? Did any of you ever see me with a sad face? And how do I meet with those whom you are afraid of and admire? Do I not treat them like slaves? Who, when he sees me, does not think that he sees his king and master?"—EP

20. If you think I live the life of an animal just because I need and use only a few things, that argument leads you to the conclusion that the gods are even lower than animals are since the gods have no needs at all.... The gods have no needs, and those men who have the fewest needs are nearest the gods.—LS

21. *A brief description of the Cynic:* You wear a beard and let your hair grow. You eschew shirts, exhibit your skin, and your feet are bare. You choose a wandering, outcast, beastly life. Unlike other people, you make your own body the object of your severities. You go

from place to place sleeping on the hard ground where chance finds you, with the result that your old cloak, neither light nor soft nor anything to look at to begin with, is loaded down with filth. —LS

22. My prayer would be that my feet might be hoofs, like Chiron's in the story, that I might need bedding no more than the lion, and costly food no more than the dog. Let my sufficient bed be the whole earth, my house this cosmos, and my chosen food the easiest to get. —LS

23. Pointing at the colonnade of Zeus and the building that housed the sacred processional vessels, Diogenes would say that the people of Athens had furnished him with places to live. —DL

24. Antisthenes wore only one garment. He was the first to fold or double over his cloak, which was rather threadbare. He carried a staff and a leather bag. —DL

25. The old cloak, the shaggy hair, the whole outfit that you ridicule has the effect that it enables me to live a quiet life. —LS

26. A leather bag stores enough for life. —LD

27. One time Diogenes saw a child drinking out of his

hands. Consequently, he pulled the cup from his leather bag and tossed it away, saying, "A child has outdone me in frugality." Another time, when he similarly observed a child who had broken his own spoon taking up lentil soup with a hollow crust of bread, he threw away his spoon.—DL

28. I've emptied my leather bag of many heavy things. I've learned that a hollowed out loaf of bread is a plate and that the hands are a drinking cup.—LD

29. "Let the drinking cups from which we drink be of clay, small and cheap. And may our drink be spring water and our food a loaf of wheat bread, and the seasoning be salt or cardamom. I learned to eat and drink these things from Antisthenes . . . things one is quite able to find on the path leading to happiness."—LD

30. I enjoy what comes to hand, use what is cheap, and have no yearning for the elaborate and exotic.—LS

31. Get used to eating barley cakes and drinking water.—LC

32. Get used to washing in cold water, drinking water, eating nothing that has not come to you by means of toil and sweat, wearing a tattered cloak, and spending

your time on the ground. —LC

33. And coming to the place where happiness exists, I said, "Because of you, Happiness, and the greater good, I persisted in drinking water and eating cardamom and sleeping on the ground." Responding to me, Happiness said, "But rather than a hardship, I will make these things sweeter to you than the goods of wealth that human beings honor before me." —LD

34. The one who is beginning to be a Cynic should first censure himself severely and cross-examine himself, and without any self-flattery, ask himself the following questions in precise terms: whether he enjoys lavish and expensive food; whether he cannot do without a soft bed; whether he is the slave of honor and reputation; whether it is his ambition to get people to look at and admire him; and, even though it is empty, he still judges it an honor. —J

Shamelessness & Rejection

1. The Cynics, or Dogs, have their name for four reasons. . . . The second reason is that the dog is a shameless animal, and Cynics praise shamelessness as being superior to decorum and respectability.—SUDA

2. Never believe, my friend, that you are free as long as the belly rules you, and the parts below the belly, since you will then have masters who can either provide you with pleasure or deprive you. And even if you become better than these, as long as you are slave to the opinions of the many, you have not yet approached freedom or tasted its nectar. . . . I do not mean by this that we should be shameless before all men and do what should not be done. Rather, in all that we abstain from and all that we do, let us not abstain from or do anything merely because it seems to the many somehow excellent or base but because it is forbidden by reason and the god within us, that is, the mind.—J

3. One day, in the midst of others, Metrocles of Maroneia farted when he was practicing a speech. He was so despondent because of what he had done that

he shut himself up in his house, fully intending to starve himself to death. When Crates learned about this and was summoned, he visited Metrocles. First, he ate a bowl of lupin beans—*on purpose*. Then he tried to persuade Metrocles that he had done nothing bad. For it would have been a miracle if he had not, following nature, relieved himself of such a blast of wind. Finally, when Crates himself farted, he renewed Metrocles' strength, encouraging him by means of similar actions.—DL

4. *Diogenes of Sinope continued speaking about Heracles:* "To avoid creating the opinion that Heracles did only impressive and mighty deeds, he went and cleaned out the dung in the Augean stables, that immense accumulation of many years. For he thought that he should fight stubbornly and war against opinion as much as against wild beasts and wicked men."

While Diogenes spoke in this manner, many stood around and listened to his words with great pleasure. Then—possibly with this thought of Heracles in his mind—he stopped speaking and, squatting on the ground, he performed an inglorious act. Seeing this, the crowd straightway scorned him and called him crazy.—DC

5. Someone dropped a loaf of wheat bread and was

ashamed to pick it up. Seeing this, Diogenes wished to offer him a lesson, and so he tied a rope to the neck of a wine-jar and dragged it across the Ceramicus. —DL

6. From that day forward, Zeno of Citium became Crates' student. And though he was in other ways very energetic in his approach to philosophy, he was nevertheless too full of shame for Cynic shamelessness. Therefore, Crates, desiring to cure the defect in him, gave him an earthen pot full of lentil soup to carry through the Ceramicus. When Crates saw that Zeno was ashamed and tried to hide the pot of soup, he broke the pot with a blow of his staff. As Zeno fled with the lentil soup flowing down his legs, Crates said, "Why do you flee, my little Phoenician? You have suffered nothing terrible!" —DL

7. Someone wished to study philosophy with Diogenes, so he gave the man a big fish to carry and told him to follow after him. Eventually, thanks to the shame he felt, the man threw the fish away and departed. Sometime later, Diogenes encountered him, and laughing, he said, "Our friendship ended thanks to a big fish!" —DL

8. When someone asked Diogenes to tell him what to do, he led him away and gave him a half obol's worth

of cheese to carry. But the man refused. Consequently, Diogenes said, "Our friendship ended thanks to a block of cheese worth a half obol." —DL

9. Do not grieve my friend, Olympias, with the fact that I wear a tattered cloak and go about begging among human beings. For this is nothing shameful. —LD

10. Don't turn back even if, because of this Cynic way of life, people call you a dog or some other worse name. —LD

11. Diogenes once begged alms from a statue. When asked why he did this, he said, "To practice being rejected." —DL

31

REINTERPRETATION

1. When someone reminded Diogenes that the citizens of Sinope had sentenced him to exile, he said, "And I sentenced them to stay there."—DDL

2. To the Sinopians: You sentenced me to exile, but I sentence you to staying! Accordingly, you will live in Sinope while I live in Athens—which is to say, you will live among merchants, and I with Solon and those men who have liberated Greece from the Persians. . . . It is far better to be disparaged by you Sinopians than to be praised by you.—LD

3. When someone said, "Most people laugh at you," Diogenes replied, "Yes—and it is likely that asses laugh at them. But even as they pay very little attention to asses, so do I not pay attention to them."—DDL

4. It is not the city that is cheap or very expensive; rather, if one lives one way it is very expensive, and if one lives another way it is cheap. So it is with circumstances. If someone makes use of them in one way, they appear favorable and easy. But if in another way, unmanageable, annoying.—T

5. Bion puts it this way: just as when you catch a wild animal, you may be bitten, so too if you take hold of a snake by the middle, you'll be bitten, but if you do so by the throat, then nothing will happen. It's the same with circumstances, he says. If you take them one way, you may experience distress. Yet if you take them in the same way as Socrates, you will not suffer. But if in any other way, then you will feel distress, not because of circumstances but because of your own character and your own false views. —T

6. When a man said to Diogenes, "The many laugh at you," he replied, "But I am not laughed down." —DDL

32

PLAYING YOUR ROLE WELL

1. Just as a good actor must contend well for the victory with the mask and role that the playwright gives him, so also must a good man compete with the one that Fortune gives him. For Bion says that Fortune, like a playwright, sometimes gives the mask and role of a first-speaker (a leading role) and sometimes that of a second-speaker (a supporting role). And sometimes a king, and sometimes a wandering beggar. So, when you are a second-speaker, do not wish for the mask and role of a first-speaker. Otherwise, you will do something unsuitable. — T

2. Fortune, as though a playwright, makes up roles of every kind: a shipwrecked man, a beggar, an exile, a well-regarded man, and one disreputable. A good man should, therefore, contend well with whatever role that Fortune gives him. You have become shipwrecked — play the shipwreck well. From being well-off you have become poor — play the poor man well. . . . Be satisfied with any clothing, food, and service that happen to come along, as was Laertes. — T

Reason

1. Reason is commander of the soul, a noble thing, the greatest good to human beings. —LC

2. We need either reason or a bridle for the conduct of life. —DDL

3. Let one consider that reason rather than a staff, and a certain plan of life rather than a leather bag are the marks of the Cynic philosophy. —J

4. We must say that happiness resides in our minds, in the best and noblest part of us. —J

5. Let a man entrust all his affairs to reason and intelligence and steer his course by them—for this was the central point, I suppose, of Diogenes' philosophy. —J

6. Before all, the governing part of the Cynic's soul must be purer than the sun. —EP

7. In the first place, then, you must make the governing part of your soul pure. And you must make the following the plan of your life: "From now on, as

wood is to the carpenter and animal hides are to the shoemaker, my mind and thoughts will be the material with which I work." —EP

8. Turn your thoughts within yourself. Observe the preconceptions that you have—the general idea of things you have. What kind of a thing do you imagine the good to be? —EP

9. Practical wisdom is a sturdy wall that will neither fall down nor be betrayed. We must build such walls by means of our own impregnable thoughts and reasonings. —ADL

10. Because we occasionally make mistakes in practice, you advise us to change our plan and correct our principles, when in fact you behave randomly in your own affairs, never acting as a result of deliberation or reason, but always thanks to habit and appetite. You are no better than people washed around by a flood. They drift with the current, you with your appetites. —LS

11. Diogenes was asked what he could do when he was captured and put up for sale. In reply he said, "I govern men." Consequently, the man said to the crier, "Announce this man—he's good if someone wants to buy a master for himself." —DL

12. When Diogenes was sold as a slave, he endured it most nobly. He was captured by pirates under the command of Scirpalus when on a voyage to Aegina. They carried him off to Crete and put him up for sale. When the herald asked him what he knew how to do, he said, "I know how to rule men." Having said this, Diogenes pointed to a certain Corinthian man, one whose garment had a fine purple border, a man named Xeniades . . . , and he said, "Sell me to this man—he needs a master." So it was that Xeniades came to buy him. He then took him to Corinth and set him over his own children and entrusted his whole household to him. Diogenes managed his property in such a manner that Xeniades used to go around saying, "A good man possessed by a god has come into my house."—DL

13. In all that we abstain from and all that we do, let us not abstain from or do anything merely because it seems to the many somehow excellent or base but because it is forbidden by reason and the god within us, that is, the mind.—J

SUPERSTITION

1. A very superstitious man said to him, "I will split open your head with one blow." Diogenes replied, "And I will make you tremble with a sneeze from the left."—DDL*

2. Observing someone purify himself, Diogenes said, "Unhappy man! Don't you know that you cannot get rid of sins by means of purification rites any more than you can get rid of grammar errors?"—DDL

3. Diogenes would generally chide men for the way they prayed, declaring that they asked for the seemingly good rather than the truly good.—DL

4. As for those who were terrified by their dreams, Diogenes would say that they did not pay attention to what they did while they were awake but were curious busybodies about all the images they see while asleep.—DL

5. When someone criticized Diogenes for going into impure places, he said, "The sun shines into a bathroom without losing its shine."—DDL

6. When Antisthenes was being initiated into the Orphic mysteries, the priest said that whoever is initiated has a share of many good things in Hades. In response, he said, "Why, then, don't you die?" —DDL

7. Diogenes saw some temple officials leading away someone who had stolen a libation bowl belonging to the treasurers, and said, "The great thieves are leading away the little thief." —DDL

8. Diogenes of Sinope used to say that when he saw ship captains and physicians and philosophers living life, he regarded humans the wisest and most intelligent of all living beings. But when he saw interpreters of dreams and diviners, and those who paid attention to them, or those who were puffed up with their own outward appearance or wealth, he acknowledged that there was no more thoughtless and empty creature than a human being. —DL

---

* In the ancient world, bad omens or signs (such as bird signs) would come on the left-hand side of the one receiving the omen or sign (presumably if they were facing north). In Homer's *Odyssey*, Penelope famously takes one of her son's sneezes as an omen. Thus, Diogenes' "sneeze from the left"—a great example of his dry wit.

Death

1. I myself am only sure about one thing—that death comes after birth. Knowing this, I blow away the empty hopes that fly around the body, and I encourage you not to think too much for a human being.—LD

2. You should also consider your migration from here. You will do so if you practice dying, that is, separating the soul from the body while you are still living.—LD

3. The Cynics hazarded what is most precious in thus despising the body—this as Socrates did when he declared, and rightly, that philosophy is the practice and preparation for death.—J

4. The brave and courageous man should, like Socrates, bravely endure his death.—T

5. When someone asked Diogenes if death is something bad, he said, "How can it be bad if, when it is present, we do not feel it?"—DDL

6. We are not able to be content with our present circumstances when we devote ourselves excessively to

luxury and when we judge work a misfortune and death the worst of evils. —T

7. If you become someone who looks down on pleasure, and someone who doesn't set himself against hard work, and someone who considers equal both good and bad reputation, and someone who doesn't fear death, then it will be possible for you to do whatever you wish without suffering distress. —T

8. The body is nothing to me. Its parts are nothing to me. And death? Let it come when it chooses—either death of the whole or some part. —EP

9. You suppose yourself unfortunate. My friend, you say, will no longer supply me with friendship since he has died. . . .

Yes, *you agree*. I'm wretched because he will no longer exist.

Nor did he exist ten thousand years ago! Nor in Trojan times! Nor even in the time of your great-grandfathers! And yet you are not grieved by this; rather, you are displeased that he will not exist in times to come.

Since I have been robbed of the intimate friendship I had with him. . . .

But this was true when he was abroad on business. Or away with the military on campaign. Or when he was serving as ambassador. Or off sacrificing.

10. To Hipparchia: Return with speed. You can still catch Diogenes while he is living—for he is already near the end of his life. Return, then, so that you can take leave of him with an embrace and come to know what philosophy may do in the most fearful circumstances.—LC

Part 4

THE CYNIC MISSION

"The true Cynic . . . must know that he is Zeus' messenger sent to human beings regarding good and bad things."

—Epictetus

"We should not profess and promise much and then practice what is not sufficient. Rather, we should demonstrate that our lives correspond with our words."

—Diogenes of Sinope

Mission—Admonishing & Helping Others

1. The true Cynic . . . must know that he is Zeus' messenger sent to human beings regarding good and bad things, to show them that they have wandered and are seeking the substance of what is good and what is bad where it is not. —EP

2. Just as the good physician should go and offer his services where the sick are most numerous, so, Diogenes said, the man of wisdom should take up his abode where fools are found in great numbers in order to convict them of their folly and correct them. —DC

3. We should not profess and promise much and then practice what is not sufficient. Rather, we should demonstrate that our lives correspond with our words. This is what I attempt to do in my own case—what I hope to be a witness of. *And I am not only thinking of others.* I am speaking of my own soul, whose notice I cannot escape when I miss the mark. —LD

4. When Antisthenes was reproached for keeping company with worthless men, he declared, "And physicians are also with the ill without becoming ill." —ADL

5. The Cynic is the father of all men—men are his sons and women are his daughters. So it is that he carefully visits everyone, so well does he care for all. Do you think that it is from idle impertinence that he admonishes those whom he meets? He does it as a father, as a brother, and as the minister of the father of all, the minister of Zeus.—EP

6. What is Caesar to a Cynic, or what is a proconsul, or what is any other, except the one who sent the Cynic down here, the one he serves—namely Zeus? Does he call upon any other one than Zeus? Is he not convinced that whatever he suffers, it is Zeus who is exercising him?—EP

7. Crates, the well-known disciple of Diogenes, was honored at Athens by the men of his own day as though he had been a household god. No house was ever closed to him, no head of a family ever had so close a secret as to regard Crates as an inconvenient intruder. He was always welcome. There was never a quarrel, never a grievance between family members that he was not accepted as the mediator and his word as law.—AP

8. When Crates' friends gave a feast, he used to go, whether invited or not, and would reconcile his

nearest friends if he learned that they had quarreled.—J

9. When reproving his friends, Crates used to admonish them not harshly but with a charming manner, and not so as to seem to persecute those whom he wished to correct but as if he wished to be of use both to them and to those listening.—J

10. Diogenes also gave his time to anyone who wished to talk with him, remarking that he was surprised by the fact that if he had claimed to be a physician for the teeth, everybody would flock to him who needed to have a tooth pulled. Yes, and by Zeus, if he had professed to treat the eyes, all who were suffering from sore eyes would present themselves. And similarly, if he had claimed to know of a medicine for diseases of the spleen or for gout or for a runny nose. But when he declared that all who followed his treatment would be relieved of ignorance, wickedness, and licentiousness, not one man would listen to him or seek to be cured by him—no matter how much richer he might become thereby. It was as though they were less inconvenienced by these spiritual complaints than by the other kind. Or as though it were worse for them to suffer from an enlarged spleen or a decayed tooth than from a soul that is foolish, ignorant, cowardly, rash,

pleasure-loving, unfree, prone to anger, unkind, and wicked—in fact, utterly corrupt.—DC

11. I called on the Cynic Antisthenes to show to us the paths that lead to happiness. . . .

Quite readily, he stood from his chair and led us into the city, straight through it to the acropolis. And when we had drawn near, he showed us two paths leading upward. The one is short, steep and troublesome; the other is long, smooth and easy.

When he brought us down, he said, "Such are the paths leading up to the acropolis. And such are the paths leading to happiness. Choose the path as you wish, and I will guide you."—LD

12. It is better to know the means by which humans are instructed to do right and act honestly than to know the means by which they are forced to do no wrong.—LC

CITIZENSHIP & POLITICAL INVOLVEMENT

1. When someone asked him where he came from, Diogenes said, "I am a citizen of the world."—DDL

2. The only true citizenship is that which is a citizenship in the whole cosmos.—DDL

3. If you will, ask me if a Cynic will engage in the administration of the state. You knob! Are you searching for a greater form of administration than that in which the Cynic is already engaged? Are you asking whether he will appear among the Athenians and say something about the revenues and the supplies, the one who must talk with all men alike, with Athenians, Corinthians, and Romans—yet not about supplies or revenues or peace or war, but about happiness and unhappiness, about good fortune and bad fortune, about slavery and freedom?—EP

4. Cynics concerned themselves with other men only insofar as they understood that man is by nature a social and political animal. And so they benefited their fellow citizens not only by serving as an example but by their conversation as well.—J

Frankness & Freedom of Speech

1. When someone asked Diogenes what was the most beautiful thing among men, he said, "Freedom of speech." —DDL

2. One day, when Diogenes was sitting in the sun nearby the Craneum grove of Corinth, Alexander stood over him and said, "Ask me for anything you desire." Diogenes replied, "I would like you to stop blocking the light." —DDL

3. The one who wishes to be a Cynic philosopher must not employ frank speech until he has first demonstrated how much he is worth—as I believe was the case with Crates and Diogenes. —J

4. It is the Cynic's responsibility, then, to be able with a loud voice, if the occasion arises, and appearing on the tragic stage, to say like Socrates: "Where are you hurrying? What are you doing, you miserable men? Like blind people you are wandering up and down. You are going by another road and have left the true road. You search for prosperity and happiness where they are not. —EP

Delusion, Vanity, Emptiness

1. He who is beginning to be a Cynic should first censure himself severely and cross-examine himself, and without any self-flattery ask himself the following questions in precise terms: whether he enjoys lavish and expensive food; whether he cannot do without a soft bed; whether he is the slave of honor and reputation; whether it is his ambition to get people to look at and admire him; and, even though it is empty, he still judges it an honor. —J

2. Diogenes of Sinope used to say that when he saw ship captains and physicians and philosophers living life, he regarded humans the wisest and most intelligent of all living beings. But when he saw interpreters of dreams and diviners, and those who paid attention to them, or those who were puffed up with their own outward appearance or wealth, he acknowledged that there was no more thoughtless and empty creature than a human being. —DL

3. Monimus said that all opinion is vanity. —DL

4. Diogenes of Sinope said, "Heracles found

Prometheus, whom I take to have been a sort of sophist, being destroyed by popular opinion since his liver swelled and grew whenever he was praised and shriveled up when he was censured. So Heracles took pity on him, frightened off the smoke-like eagle, and thus relieved him of his vanity and inordinate ambition. And straightway he disappeared after making him whole." —DC

5. For me life is so unreliable and uncertain that I cannot rely on lasting here until I finish writing this letter to you. Regardless, a leather bag stores enough for it. . . . I myself am only sure about one thing—that death comes after birth. Knowing this, I blow away the empty hopes that fly around the body, and I encourage you not to think too much for a human being. —LD

6. *Diogenes of Sinope said, "In conformity with self-sufficiency and simplicity,* the soul has been purified of vice and has been released from empty opinion. It has cast out immoderate desires and has been taught to speak the truth and to show contempt for other false things. If you are not persuaded by this, then practice the love of pleasure and tease us for not knowing much." —LD

7. The chief men of Cynicism were Antisthenes, Diogenes, and Crates. The goal of their lives was, I think,

to know themselves, to be aware of empty opinions, and to lay hold of truth with their whole understanding. This is so because truth—both for gods and men—is the beginning of every good thing. —J

ALTERING THE CURRENCY

1. Diogenes granted nothing at all . . . to human custom and law; rather, he followed nature. In this way he practiced "altering the currency," which is to say he reevaluated human customs. —DL

2. Listen to the Pythian god Apollo when he counsels these two precepts, "Know Yourself," and "Alter the currency." —J

FRIENDSHIP

1. Let me speak of the most exquisite possession of all. You observe that I always have leisure, with the result that I can go and see whatever is worth seeing and hear whatever is worth hearing and—what I prize the most—I pass the whole day, untroubled by business, in Socrates' company. Like me, he does not bestow his admiration on those who count the most gold, but he spends his time with those who are pleasing to him.—AX

2. The old cloak, the shaggy hair, the whole outfit that you ridicule has the effect that it enables me to live a quiet life, doing what I want and keeping the company I wish to keep.—LS

3. Cynics recognize those who are suited to philosophy as friends, and they welcome them kindly, while they bark like dogs at those who are ill-equipped for the pursuit of wisdom.—SCHOLIA IN ARISTOTELEM

4. When brothers agree, no fortress is as strong as their common life.—ADL

5. A good man is worthy of love. Excellent men—serious men of character—are friends.—ADL

6. The Cynics teach that the wise man is worthy of love. He is a man without fault, and a friend to similar men.—DL

7. Make allies of men who are at once courageous and just.—ADL

8. Honor a just man more than a kinsman.—ADL

9. It is better to fight with a few good men against everyone who is bad than to fight with a multitude of bad men against the few who are good.—ADL

10. It is better to fall in with carrion crows than with flatterers since the one eats the dead, while the other devours the living.—ADL

11. All things belong to the gods. The wise are friends of the gods, and friends hold all things in common. Therefore, all things belong to the wise.—DDL

12. We should hold out our hands to our friends without closing the fingers.—DDL

13. This simple kind of wealth makes people generous. My friend Socrates here and I are examples. For Socrates, from whom I acquired this wealth of mine, did not come to my relief limiting it by number and weight, but he gave me all that I could carry. And as for me, I am now stingy with no one; rather, I openly display my abundance to all my friends and share my soul wealth with anyone who desires it. —AX

Miscellaneous Sayings & Anecdotes

1. It is ridiculous that men sacrifice to the gods to ensure health, but during the sacrifice they feast in a manner that harms health. —DDL

2. Alexander the Great is reported to have said, "If I had not been Alexander, I would have liked to have been Diogenes." —DL

3. When Diogenes came to Athens, he approached Antisthenes. The latter sent him away since he did not accept students. Still, Diogenes wore Antisthenes down by his sheer persistence. One day, when Antisthenes raised his staff against him, the student offered his head to him and said, "Strike it!—you will find no wood hard enough to keep me away from you as long as I think you have something to say." —DL

4. Seek wise men, even if you have to go to the ends of the earth. —LC

5. My dear students, you are midway between the gods and irrational animals. —LC

6. Hold fast to the ancients. —LC

7. When a man demonstrated by a syllogism that he had horns, Diogenes touched his forehead and said, "I don't see them." Similarly, when someone declared that there is no such thing as motion, Diogenes stood up and walked back and forth. —DDL

8. When Diogenes was asked why athletes are so senseless, he said, "Because they are built up of swine and cattle flesh." —DDL

9. When a friend complained to him that he had lost his notes, Antisthenes said, "You should have written them on your mind instead of on paper." —ADL

10. Antisthenes said that being "earth-born" made the Athenians no more well-born than spiral-shelled snails or wingless locusts. —DL

11. Antisthenes used to advise the Athenians to vote that asses are horses. When they judged the proposal irrational, he said, "And yet there are generals among you who have had no training but are merely elected." —DDL

12. To the youth who was posing fantastically as an

artist's model, Antisthenes said, "Tell me, if the bronze could speak, on what do you believe it would pride itself most?" The youth replied, "On its beauty." Antisthenes said, "Are you not, then, ashamed of taking pride in the same thing as a lifeless thing?" —ADL

13. An older boy from Pontus asked Antisthenes what he required to learn with him. The latter replied, "Bring a new book, a new writing utensil, and new writing tablets." He meant that he should bring and have on display a new mind. —DL

14. As iron is devoured by rust so are jealous people consumed by their own jealous disposition. —ADL

15. I condemn those who commend just men for being above their property and money while being jealous of the very rich. —DDL

16. Some man had been reading aloud for a very long time, and when he drew near to the end of the scroll and pointed to a space with no writing, Diogenes said, "Take courage, men. I see land." —DDL

17. A young man was playing kottabos* in the baths. Diogenes said to him, "The better you play, the worse it is for you." —DDL

18. When Diogenes was asked why gold is pale, he said, "Because gold has so many people plotting against it." —DDL

19. When Diogenes was returning from Lacedaemon to Athens, someone asked him, "Where are you coming from and where are you going?" He replied, "I'm going from the men's part of the house to the women's part." —DDL

20. Crates used to say that it was impossible to find a flawless person, just as pomegranates always have one rotten seed. —DL

21. When someone asked him what the proper time for lunch was, Diogenes said, "If you're a rich man, whenever you want. If you're poor, whenever you can." —DL

22. To a man who had his servant put on his shoes, Diogenes said, "You won't be happy until he wipes your nose. And that won't happen until your hands are disabled." —DDL

23. Seeing a profligate man eating olives in a tavern, Diogenes said, "If you had eaten breakfast in this way, you would not be eating dinner is this way." —DL

24. One should neither marry nor have children since our kind, humankind, is weak, and marriage and children overload human weakness with troubles. —LD

25. The beard is man's ornament—like the lion's or the horse's mane, to whom god had added a certain grace of splendor and adornment just as he added the beard to men —LS

26. When Antisthenes was reproached because his parents were not both freemen, he said, "Neither were they both wrestlers. Even so, I am a wrestler." —ADL

27. To the one who looked down on his father in contempt, Diogenes said, "Are you not ashamed to look down on the very one without whom you would not be here to exhibit such pride?" —DDL

*Kottabos was a drinking game. The players made wishes while playing, often with an amorous or erotic intent, believing that the winner's wish would be granted.

WAYS OF PRACTICE

- A Plan of Life
Following the Cynics

- Ways of Practice
Following the Cynics

- The Cynics Cave Sparks
(Conversation Starters
Sparked by the Cynics)

A Plan of Life
Following the Cynics

Let him who wishes to be a Cynic philosopher realize that . . . reason and a certain plan of life . . . are the marks of the Cynic philosophy.
—Julian the Roman emperor

As with any other plan, a plan of life is made to accomplish certain goals or possibly just one significant goal. Here the goal is happiness in terms of a simple life lived in harmony with nature and thus virtue.

The following plan consists of the most significant goals and practices inspired by the ancient Cynics.

1. **Do philosophy.** But when doing philosophy, realize it's not primarily about original insights or clever quips, but about *doing*, *being*, *living*. Philosophy is a change of character, an alteration of life.

2. **Live according to nature, according to virtue.** Turn down the noise of convention, of human customs. Hear instead the hum of nature alone. Observe how animals behave, how they are content. Nature directs us to what is actually virtuous rather than merely *apparently* virtuous. Accordingly, we may discover what is good, bad, and indifferent; and so,

we are able to "alter the currency," to shift our conception of what is truly valuable and what is not.

3. **Cultivate shamelessness.** Be a dog. Imitate the behavior and attitude of dogs. Do what needs to be done, what *you* need to do, without worrying about what others will think or say. Practice shamelessness. Do something usually judged embarrassing today.

4. **Exercise frankness.** Don't hide your thoughts; don't let your speech imprison you. Don't be fake, wearing a sham speech-mask that is not you. Speak freely to be free and to aid others in the same.

5. **Build soul wealth.** Understand that happiness is a matter of internal goods such as contentment and inner strength rather than external things like fine clothing, gourmet food, a "good" reputation, political office, wealth, and other possessions. Soul wealth is built by fostering soul health—by engaging in specific practices related to following the Cynic plan of life.

6. **Keep freedom in mind.** Know that everything we do has the potential to liberate or enslave us. Ask yourself: will *having* something release or restrict me? Will *doing* something liberate or bind me? Will *feeling* or *thinking* something free or fetter me? Will *saying*

something help or hinder me? The Cynic always moves toward freedom and flees enslavement—whether for himself or others.

7. **Turn down the voice of popular opinion.** Live beyond the waves of fashion and the constant urge for popularity, fame, and a "good" reputation. Practice obscurity. Practice rejection.

8. **Practice endurance.** Embrace toil, hardship, and suffering. When necessary, stand your ground against the allure of pleasure. Practice in the manner of Diogenes, who walked barefoot in the snow, rolled in the hot sand, bravely battled a fever, and begged alms from a statue in order to practice rejection.

9. **Reduce your desires.** Know that desire always leaves one desiring more. As such, desire indicates dissatisfaction. By reducing desires, we are able to reduce dissatisfaction. Said another way, desire reduction increases satisfaction. Reduce your desires, therefore, to expand your overall sense of contentment and satisfaction. Get used to saying, "No." Practice contentment.

10. **Develop self-control.** Desire reduction is essential for the Cynic development of self-control. The reason

is simple: self-control increases as desire decreases. Consequently, as you practice reducing your desires, know you are simultaneously establishing self-control. Said positively, contentment aids (self-)containment or self-restraint.

11. **Strive for self-sufficiency.** Be independent—of life conditions, of others, of desires or wants that are hard to satisfy. Focus on what is necessary. Be content with what is near to hand and easy to procure. What are you? Who do you know? What do you have? What are you doing? What do you feel? May that be sufficient. Say, "I am satisfied with —."

12. **Live simply.** Living frugally or simply follows upon the practices of desire reduction and self-sufficiency. Wear simple clothes. Reduce your possessions. Eat basic fare. Drink water. Imitate Socrates, who rejoiced in all the things he could go without while walking through the market.

WAYS OF PRACTICE
FOLLOWING THE CYNICS

THE FOLLOWING WAYS of practice are offered with the goal of applying the wisdom and ways of the Cynics to your own life. For similar exercises and more (significantly expanded with ample space for reflection), pick up the Cave's *The Cynics Workbook & Journal*.

> **PRACTICE 1** • Seeking Freedom and Avoiding Enslavement

"Diogenes declared that his manner of life was the same as that of Heracles. He preferred freedom more than everything else." —Diogenes Laertius

CONTEMPLATION • Ancient Greeks had a strong taste for freedom. The ancient Greek historian Herodotus tells us about their struggle for freedom against the Persians—a freedom secured after more than a decade of on-and-off war.

What about me? What am I willing to do for freedom?

In what ways am I unfree (enslaved) in any way?

In what ways am I free? *From* things? *To do* things?

DECLARATION OF INDEPENDENCE & PRACTICE PLAN

Assuming you are unfree or enslaved (at least in some ways), take a moment to declare your independence from whatever is holding you back, hampering you, enslaving you. Then write down two things you can do to practice freedom relative to these things. Be specific and concrete.

Declaration of Independence

Freedom Practice Plan

1.

2.

> **PRACTICE 2** • Living Satisfied
> and Practicing Contentment

In response to the man who asked, "What will it mean for me to do philosophy?" Crates said, "You will live satisfied with what you have, neither desiring what is absent nor being displeased with whatever comes your way." —Teles of Megara

"Do not be distressed, father, that I call myself a dog. . . . Instead, be delighted that your son is content with little."
—Diogenes of Sinope

RATE YOURSELF • On a scale of one to ten, ten being the most, how content are you? Circle your contentment number.

1   2   3   4   5   6   7   8   9   10

"We are not able to be content with our present circumstances when we devote ourselves excessively to luxury and when we judge work a misfortune and death the worst of evils." —Teles of Megara

SELF CHECK • Consider the following points and questions.

What is contentment? Is it more of a feeling or a judgment?

_____

_____

Echoing the above quote, "I am <u>not able</u> to be content with my present circumstances when" . . . what?

Conversely, "I am <u>able</u> to be content with my present circumstances when" . . . what?

CONTENTMENT PLAN • List **two things** you struggle to be content or satisfied with. Name two specific and concrete ways you can **practice contentment** with each. You may practice with the way you feel, what you think, how you react, what you say, and what you do—or in some other way.

Thing 1

Contentment practice 1

Thing 2

Contentment practice 2

THE CYNICS CAVE SPARKS
(CONVERSATIONS STARTERS SPARKED BY THE CYNICS)

Read the following Cave Sparks or Conversation Starters from the Cynics. Then discuss the connected Cave Spark Questions—with your friends, family, colleagues, class, youth group, or others.

ONE ▪ THE PRACTICE OF DAILY DEEDS

"Long is the path that leads to happiness through words alone. But the path that leads to happiness through the practice of daily deeds is short." —Crates of Thebes

1. Is it possible to be happy by merely talking about happiness—that is, on the path of "words alone"? What role (if any) can words play in experiencing happiness?

2. Is happiness something that we must practice? If so, why and how? If not, why not?

3. What specific daily practices can we engage in to walk along the path that leads to happiness? Are big or small steps (or practices) more beneficial? Explain.

TWO ▪ THE SOURCE OF MANY EVILS

"May I have no need—I nor any that I call friend—for gold and silver. For every human misfortune is generated by a longing for these—civil strife and wars, conspiracies and slaughters. The fountain of them all is a longing for more." —an anonymous Cynic

1. Why do people say that gold and silver is valuable? Are they valuable in themselves?

2. What role does wealth ("gold and silver") play relative to the various bad things ("evils") we humans experience? What about good things?

3. What things are truly valuable? What must humans have for a good life?

Three ▪ Enslavement to Desire

"Bad men obey their desires as house slaves obey their masters." —Diogenes of Sinope

1. What is desire? Are there bad desires? If so, what makes them bad? What sort of desires do "bad people" have? Give three examples.

2. What is obedience? What motivates a slave or servant to obey his or her master or boss? What negative things? What positive things? Does Diogenes' analogy work?

3. Does an alcoholic obey his or her desire for alcohol like a slave obeys his or her master? What other desires are similar? Have you ever experienced such a desire?

Will you help the Cave? Here's how . . .

- **Talk** to friends and family about Cave books and other offerings at the Cave (www.theclassicscave.com).
- Leave a **positive review** online.
- **Write us** at contact@theclassicscave.com to let us know how you've benefited from our work.

THE CLASSICS CAVE is a small, shoestring operation, on fire to spread the wisdom and ways of ancient literature. We **rely on you**, the friend of the Cave, to let people know how you liked and benefited from what we're doing. We also **depend on you to improve our books**. Did you see something that requires editing? Something we got wrong? Something we need to add? Despite our great effort and care to get everything right, it happens. So please **let us know** by emailing us at contact@theclassicscave.com. Otherwise, **support our mission** to spread the wisdom and ways of ancient literature by reading more from the Cave and visiting our ever-growing collection of online material at www.theclassicscave.com.

Read and enjoy more from the Cynics at the Cave.

Looking for the **best books** ever?
And new ways to read and benefit from them?

Hunting for **wisdom** and **ways** that
are time-tested and people-approved?

READ A CAVE BOOK

VISIT THE CAVE ONLINE
www.theclassicscave.com

When you read a Cave book, an ancient classic,
you'll have a better idea about where you're
going in life and how to get there.

You'll feel smarter. Be wiser.
And if you practice what you've encountered,
you'll live a better life. Be a little happier.

Choose a book from one of **our series**. The Cave Best of Series. The Cave Wisdom & Way Series. The Cave Workbook & Journal Series. The Cave Sparks (Conversation Starters) Series. **You'll be glad you did!**

www.theclassicscave.com

Printed in Great Britain
by Amazon